Gilbert Harrison

Travels in various parts of Europe during the years 1888, 1889, 1890

Being a short and practical account

Gilbert Harrison

Travels in various parts of Europe during the years 1888, 1889, 1890
Being a short and practical account

ISBN/EAN: 9783337207144

Printed in Europe, USA, Canada, Australia, Japan

Cover: Foto ©Andreas Hilbeck / pixelio.de

More available books at **www.hansebooks.com**

OPORTO.

TRAVELS

IN

VARIOUS PARTS OF EUROPE

During the Years 1888, 1889, and 1890:

BEING

A SHORT

AND

PRACTICAL ACCOUNT,

BY

GILBERT H. W. HARRISON.

(With 24 Illustrations)

LONDON:

BEMROSE & SONS, 23 OLD BAILEY: and DERBY.

[ALL RIGHTS RESERVED.]

1891.

LIST OF ILLUSTRATIONS.

1	OPORTO	Frontispiece
2	GENERAL VIEW OF AMBLESIDE	To face page 14
3	RYDAL MOUNT, AS IT IS	,, ,, 16
4	INNSBRUCK	,, ,, 24
5	MERAN	,, ,, 25
6	SALZBURG	,, ,, 26
7	ST. STEPHEN'S CATHEDRAL, WIEN	page 27
8	VIEW FROM HOTEL HUNGARIA, BUDAPEST	,, 30
9	SZEGED	,, 32
10	ADAKALEH, OR NEW ORSOVA	,, 34
11	KRONKAPELLE AT ORSOVA	,, 36
12	CURSALON, MEHADIA	,, 37
13	TRINKGROTTE, CURSALON AND GISELLA PARK, MEHADIA	,, 38
14	ABBAZIA	,, 42
15	ARCADE AT MILAN	,, 45
16	A WOMAN OF ARLES	To face page 52
17	AVIGNON	,, ,, 53
18	ZARAGOZA CATHEDRAL	Page 55
19	SALAMANCA CATHEDRAL	,, 58
20	VIEW OF LISBON	To face page 62
21	GENERAL VIEW OF CINTRA	,, ,, 63
22	CADIZ	Page 68
23	GENERAL VIEW OF CORDOVA	,, 72
24	INTERIOR OF CORDOVA CATHEDRAL	,, 74

CONTENTS.

CHAPTER I.
                                                                             PAGE

NORTH OF PORTUGAL. 1
    Braga beggars—Chicken Broth made of Bacon—Wet weather—Caldas de Vizella.

CHAPTER II.

EAST COAST OF ENGLAND. 3
    Hunstanton—Good Beer at King's Lynn—Yarmouth—Cromer—Felixstowe—Clacton-on-Sea — Margate—Salubrity of Climate Bathing arrangements—Clever Sculptor — Numerous amusements—Hotels—Danger on Cliff—High price of Coals.

CHAPTER III.

JOURNEY TO DRESDEN 6
    Stupid arrangements about tickets..Amusing incident—Stupidity about registering luggage at Dover—Cold weather.

CHAPTER IV.

DESCRIPTION OF DRESDEN 8
    Very changeable climate—Fine opera—Grand sacred Music.—Good classical music—Numerous Musical *Cafés*—Churches—Hotels—Life at a *pension*—Fondness of Germans for pork—Not many Jews—Absence of beggars—Nasty coal burnt—Skating—Large number of young ladies.

CHAPTER V.

LEIPZIG 13
    Gewandhaus concert—Scarcity of pretty faces—Auerbach's Keller — Picture Gallery — New Monument — Saxon Switzerland—Severe weather, followed by thaw—Hurried journey to England

CHAPTER VI.

AMBLESIDE 15

CHAPTER VII.

SEASCALE 16

CHAPTER VIII.

SHAP WELLS, SILLOTH AND GILSLAND 17

CHAPTER IX.

NORTH-EAST COAST OF BRITAIN 18
Edinburgh—Uncomfortable hotel there—North Berwick—Dunbar—Berwick-on-Tweed—Exhilarating air—Tynemouth—Seaweed used as food—Durham—Poor music in Cathedral.

CHAPTER X.

JOURNEY TO PARIS. 21
Uncomfortable travelling—Channel Tunnel.

CHAPTER XI.

FROM PARIS TO WIEN 24
Paris Exhibition—Excellent Hungarian music—Crowded state of City—Departure for Austria—Innsbruck—Meran—Floods and avalanches—Salzburg — Fine band at Cursalon — Wien — "Beautiful Blue Danube"—Badly paved streets—Poor cooking—Excellent Violinists—Elegance of Females.

CHAPTER XII.

BUDAPEST 27
Departure for Budapest—Danube scenery—Rascally omnibus conductor — Grand Hotel Hungaria — Buda — Fine bridge across river—Flaxen haired children—Blocksburg—Blocksbad—Other baths—Margit Isle—Description of hotel at Pest.

CHAPTER XIII.

TOUR IN HUNGARY 32
Szeged — The Alföld—Bazias --- Scenery on Danube between Bazias and Orsova—Beauty of Orsova—Good wine—Fine organ playing — New Orsova — Verciorova — Adventure at Hungarian guardhouse—Kronkapelle—Mehadia—Loveliness of scenery — Temesvar — Liveliness of hotel there — Ruster Ausbruch — Fascinating music of Gipsy band— Excellent omelettes and coffee in Hungary—Return to Pest—A mighty man of valour—Hungarians and Austrians not so highly educated as North Germans—Boy waiters—Curious customs in hotels—Good wines—Cheap soup—Cheap postage—Cheap railway travelling.

CHAPTER XIV.

FROM PEST TO GÖRZ 41
Regret at having to leave Pest—Kanizsa—Agram—Uninteresting place—Karlstadt—Fiume—Good military band—Great warmth of climate—Abbazia—Expensive hotel—Lovely Bay—Adelsberg—Visit to newly discovered grotto—Excitable Hungarian—Miramar Castle—Trieste—Drunken men—Görz—Good wine.

CHAPTER XV.

NORTHERN ITALY 45
Difference between Austria and Italy—Padua—Splendid statue of Garibaldi— Nasty coffee—Lake Garda—Milan—Genoa—Heavy rain—Hotel Isotta—Plain women—Men as chambermaids—Dearness of soup—Bougie swindle.

CHAPTER XVI.

CRUELTY TO ANIMALS 49
Sport—Vivisection.

CHAPTER XVII.

SOUTH OF FRANCE AND NORTH OF SPAIN 52
Ventimiglia—Mosquitos—Loveliness of Riviera—Marseille—Arles—Avignon—Villainously paved streets at these two latter towns. Cette—Barcelona—Lerida—Zaragoza—Dearness of omnibuses in Spain—Bad butter—Bad sanitation—Numbers of beggars—Grand cathedral—Grand *Café*—Leaning tower—Castejon—Living very cheap and good—Pleasant travelling companions.

CHAPTER XVIII.

SOME OLD SPANISH TOWNS 57
Burgos — Strong wine — Cathedral — Gregorian chanting — Valladolid — Barrel Organ — Cold travelling — Salamanca — Beautiful cathedral—Ciudad Rodrigo—Extraordinary hotel—Nasty food—Journey with donkeys—Fuentes de Oñoro—Dirty railway carriage—Arrival at Oporto.

CHAPTER XIX.

SOUTH OF PORTUGAL 62
Aveiro—Lisbon—Numerous funerals—Poor hotel accommodation—Extraordinary appetites of Portuguese—Bad smelling cities—Cintra—Cape Roca—Setubal—Filthy hotel there—Beja—Faro Dirty place—Villa Real—Clean inn.

CHAPTER XX.

SOUTH-WEST ANDALUCIA 66
Ayamonte—Lepe—Beauty of women—Cartaja—Good wine—Huelva—Excellence of hotel there—Salubrity of climate—Rabida Convent—Christopher Columbus.

CHAPTER XXI.

SOME INTERESTING PLACES IN ANDALUCIA 68
Seville—Cadiz—Multitudes of Turkeys there—Jerez; delicious wine—Seville again : quantities of barber's shops. Hotel de Madrid very comfortable—Spanish management of hotels to be recommended—From Seville to Malaga—Grand scenery near Bobadilla—Extraordinary warmth of climate—Visit to a *Café Chantant*—Arrival at Cordova.

CHAPTER XXII.

CORDOVA, SEVILLE AND MERIDA 72
Cordova; Bacalhao—The attack on Dr. Middleton—Adventure of Author with a would-be guide—Narrowness of streets—Mosque — Desirability of learning modern languages — Picturesque route to Seville—Almodovar—Seville once more—Sucursal of H. Madrid—Visit to a *Café chantant*—Visit to tobacco manufactory — English holding peculiar views of matrimony—The fashionable promenade—Youthful clergyman—Display of beauty on DELICIAS—Amusing anecdotes about hair-cutter and tailor—*Times* newspaper—Drying clothes on house-tops —Bull-fighting —Muzzling donkeys — Mildness of climate—Fine wild scenery—Merida : Pretty girls at FONDA—Amusing incident at dinner.

CONCLUDING REMARKS				.. ..	80
APPENDIX	I.—AVIGNON ..			.. ..	81
,,	II.—BARCELONA			.. ..	83
,,	III.—LERIDA ..	..		.. ..	85
,,	IV.—ZARAGOZA	..	..	.. ..	86
,,	V.—SALAMANCA	..	..	.. ..	88
,,	VI.—Extract from CHAUCER'S PROLOGUE...			..	89

ERRATA.

Page 23—2nd line from top, for *Martinets* read *Marionettes*.

,, 50—10th line from bottom, insert semicolon after *called in*, and delete comma after *at Parliamentary Elections*.

,, 54—1st line, insert semicolon after *and not far from the water*, and in second line, after *main street*, a comma.

,, 571—9th line from bottom, for *Hotel Giglo* read *Hotel Siglo*.

,, 57—8th line from bottom, for *Comeras* read *Comercio*.

,, 64—10th line from top, for *Loule* and *Loulé*.

,, 73—16th line from bottom, for *so* read *to*.

,, 75—19th and 20th lines from bottom, read *the screaming and yelling that take place are most discordant*.

,, 83—10th line from bottom, for *beseiged* read *besieged*.

,, 85—After " LERIDA " delete " CARTHAGENIAN."

,, 85—6th line from top, for *Cipio* read *Scipio*.

,, 85—7th line from top, for *Carthegenian* read *Carthagenian*.

,, 88—Lines 6 and 7 from bottom, for *continous* and *Aristotl*, read *continues* and *Aristotle*.

Chapter xv.—*Lepe, Cartaja*, refer to Appendix vi.

CHAPTER I.

NORTH OF PORTUGAL.

N April, being at OPORTO I made a little excursion, having for a companion an invalid brother-in-law. The weather was showery, which appears to be frequently the case at that time of the year in that part of the world, and I was for postponing the trip, but my brother-in-law seemed to reckon more by the barometer (which must have been out of repair, as it kept pointing more and more towards fair weather, whilst the weather was in reality getting wetter and wetter) than by what he saw of the rain with his eyes, and was bent upon starting notwithstanding the wet; so off we set first to BRAGA notorious for its beggars, and certainly they are a disgusting sight! If they possess deformities they make the most of them—displaying them for the purpose of exciting sympathy and obtaining alms, and if they possess no deformities then report has it that they malinger and create them in order the more to excite compassion.

From BRAGA station we went by steam tram to the foot of BOM JESUS where we took the hydraulic lift. This place the reader will find mentioned in a little pamphlet written by me, and entitled *Winter and Spring in Spain and Portugal*, which may be obtained of Mr. F. Dugon, 24, Worship Street, London, E.C. The rain continued, and after taking a drive by the river Cavado, a fine broad stream, we set off by train to VALENÇA, the frontier town of Portugal. We put up at a dirty little inn, and the food was miserable stuff. The next day we took a drive across the fine bridge over the river Minho into Spain. TUY is the name of the frontier town on the Spanish side: this place also is mentioned in the pamphlet referred to above. I was much amused by a little incident that occurred at VALENÇA railway station. We had sometime to wait, and I attempted some luncheon; having a predilection for pork I demanded some and they brought me a thick lump of boiled fat bacon. My brother-in-law who was a martyr to indigestion afterwards asked for some chicken broth, and when it was placed before him, there could be no mistake about it, it had been made out of the remains of my bacon, and the invalid waxed full of wrath! Returning we stayed at CAMINHA, passing on the way a most beautiful village called CERVEIRA. The inn at CAMINHA was clean and comfortable, and we fared considerably better than we had done at VALENÇA; but the rain still continued and we went on to VIANNA. Here a friend took upon himself to entertain us, and drove us back as far as ANCORA where we spent two wet days, afterwards returning to OPORTO.

Early in May I re-visited that beautiful spot, VIZELLA, which I have mentioned in my pamphlet referred to above. I know no lovelier route by rail than that alongside the river VIZELLA, the stream is so clear and crystal, frequently being crossed by old moss and ivy-covered bridges, the birds sing so sweetly, the sun beams so cheerfully as we wind our way languidly along as if life were but a dream, no necessity for hurry. As these Portuguese trains have only single lines of rail to run on, considerable delay is often caused at shunting places, for if one train is behind time it puts all the others out.

CHAPTER II.

EAST COAST OF ENGLAND.

I WILL now describe a tour on the East Coast of England, starting from HUNSTANTON, which is situated on the WASH. I found this a pretty place with splendid sands, but somewhat dull, and travelled on to GREAT YARMOUTH by way of KING'S LYNN, a clean old-fashioned town, where I enjoyed some excellent ale which had been brewed in the town. I found YARMOUTH to be a large noisy over-crowded place, possessing a very grand church, said to be the largest in England. The sands here are very soft and the climate is cold, subject to east winds. From YARMOUTH I visited CROMER, a most beautiful place in my estimation, and LOWESTOFT which I did not care for.

FELIXSTOWE was the next place I visited. The beach is not good, too shingly, but the bathing-machines are commodious. A great many bathing-tents are taken by visitors on hire. These extend for a considerable distance along the beach, and are used in the afternoons as lounges where people read or converse.

Previously this same year I had paid a visit to CLACTON-ON-SEA. The season had scarcely begun. I stayed at the Royal Hotel and found it very comfortable. The bathing-machines at CLACTON were roomy, but the beach was not particularly good. This place being on the East Coast, but having a Southern aspect, the climate is bracing though mild. I should consider it a rising place, likely some day to rival MARGATE in the Londoners' idea, being only a little over two hours from the Metropolis.

I now come to that most amusing of all the seaside resorts I know, MARGATE. This place possesses a bracing climate and low death rate. It is said to be the sunniest and driest seaside resort in Great Britain. The aspect is due north; and in spring the east and north winds are most cutting; at other times of the year, however, there is not much cause for complaint, and the natives declare that in winter they are almost free from snow and frost, whilst in summer, although there are no trees to afford shelter, and the chalk cliffs render the place very glaring, the cool breezes tend to neutralise the effects of the sun and warm air. There may be said to be two MARGATES—old MARGATE, near the railway station and pier, which is the part that trippers frequent, and the new part of the town beyond the fort which is called Cliftonville, the extreme end of which goes by the name of New-town. It is on these cliffs that the best houses are situated. Cuttings have been made through the cliffs for people to approach the shore and there are two bathing establishments close to each other both belonging to the same family, although Mrs. Charlotte Pettman, the owner and manageress of one establishment, has no business connection with her brother, the proprietor of the other. The bathing grounds are thus marked out—each possesses a place for ladies only and a place for both sexes. This arrangement is perhaps rather hard on some prudish members of the male persuasion. It is a saying that the good-looking girls frequent the promiscuous bathing-place whilst those less favoured by nature resort to the place for ladies only. Bathing goes on from 6 a.m. to 6 p.m. every day, Sundays included, and tickets can be purchased for 4/6 the dozen, but each bather is expected to pay 1d. to the man who brings him ashore in the cart, for carts are used both to convey the bathers to the machines and to bring them back again, except at high-tide when one is able to walk off the plank into one's bathing-machine. The wheels of these machines, some of them at least, stand twelve feet high. They are very strongly-built vehicles, but not as commodious as others to be found along the East Coast at the places before mentioned. A quaint bit of rhyme has been printed and pasted up in most of Mrs. Pettmann's machines. It runs thus:—

> " I pitied the dove, for my bosom was tender,
> " I pitied the sigh that she gave to the wind ;
> " But I ne'er shall forget the superlative splendour,
> " Of Charlotte's sea baths, the pride of mankind."

·The water at MARGATE is not of the clearest description and is generally cold. The sands do not extend a great distance towards the water, and cuttings have been made in the rocks for the convenience of the bathers. A quantity of seaweed sometimes collects and decomposes which is very disagreeable. The sands in the morning are crowded with nurses and children ; and niggers, organ-grinders, and others add to the general hubbub. Every year, during the height of the season, a mission is held on the sands, a harmonium is played, and the nurses and children join in the singing. This used to be under the patronage of one of the MARGATE clergy. A very talented amateur sculptor made his appearance a ew years ago and carved figures out of the cliffs. This year he sculptured a girl in bathing-costume in the act of diving into the water. This turned out to be such a success that it was protected by a boarding and a charge made to see it, the money being devoted to the MARGATE cottage hospital. No place could be better off for amusements than MARGATE. There is the Hall-by-the-sea, belonging to Mr. Sanger the circus proprietor, which has Zoological gardens and menagerie attached to it. There is a theatre for those who like to shut themselves up in its stuffy atmosphere. There are the new assembly-rooms, beautifully decorated, where dancing takes place nightly. There is the Marine Palace, where a band plays at intervals during the day, and various kinds of entertainments are given at night. There is the splendid pier, having a large refreshment-room in the centre where another band performs three times a day. There is the MARGATE town band which plays every evening on the Green on what is called "The Fort." Besides all these there is a strolling band of musicians who serenade the hotels and boarding-houses throughout the day, and play at the principal bathing hour at Briggs' baths, which are the oldest established in MARGATE. Of the hotels, the Cliftonville is the largest and has the best situation, but there are no lifts—a very great drawback in a many-storied house, and the charges, I am told, in the season are extortionate. The York is a comfortable house, but it is situated opposite the harbour in the low-lying part of MARGATE. The only other hotel I have stayed at is the Nayland Rock, conveniently situated near the London and Chatham railway station, but I did not find that the food was particularly toothsome there. The highly-situated promenade beginning at the "Fort" and extending to the Flagstaff—a mile or more in length is asphalted, but just beyond the Pettman's bathing establishments, there is no protection whatever; and as the cliff is somewhat steep and occasionally gives way, this forms a source of danger, particularly to children. I cannot understand the perversity of the local authorities in not causing a railing to be erected, especially as their attention has frequently been called to the desirability of such a thing. Another drawback to MARGATE is the high price of coals; this is caused by the Pier and Harbour Company levying heavy charges on all coals brought to the town even by land, which is an absurd anomaly. But everything during the season is expensive at MARGATE; provisions, house-rents, and lodgings, fetch enormous prices.

CHAPTER III.

JOURNEY TO DRESDEN.

ON the 17th October we left "Merry MARGATE" for DRESDEN. I had provided myself with through tickets, issued by the South Eastern Railway Company—but they were only available *via* ASHFORD, thus causing us to go a considerable distance out of the direct route, which was by DEAL to DOVER, whereas these tickets obliged us to go *via* FOLKESTONE to DOVER, a long way round.

I may as well here relate an amusing incident that occurred at MARGATE. I had occasion to go to the goods' office of the S.E.R. Company to make enquiries about sending luggage to DRESDEN.

"DRESDEN!" exclaimed the youthful clerk; "DRESDEN; why that's in China, isn't it?"

I noticed in the carriage we got at ASHFORD that there was posted up a little map of our route a capital idea that reminded me of travel in Germany. We had a smooth crossing to CALAIS in the "*Empress*," but a slow one, the steward informing me that these boats, although capable of doing the passage in just over the hour, usually take one-and-a-quarter hours or more. The line of rail to BRUSSELS is exceptionally uninteresting. We pass, however, one very fine station, TOURNAI. There are two stations at BRUSSELS; first comes the *Midi* and then the *Nord*. We wished to go to the *Nord* as that is where the trains running to COLOGNE start from—but at DOVER they would not register our luggage further than to the *Midi*, an idiotic piece of business—the consequence of which was that we had to stay all night at the *Hotel de l'Industrie*, close to the *Midi* station, and drive the next morning through the city to the other station. (Our train of the previous evening went to both stations, whereas we found no morning train to suit us.) After a night at COLOGNE (*German, Köln* or *Cöln*) and a glimpse at its glorious cathedral, which by the way our Swiss nurse said she did not care to see as there was quite as good an one at EINSEDELN, in her country—we went on to HANNOVER. The weather was bitterly cold, but the railway carriages were so comfortably warmed that we did not feel it. What uncomfortable beds one finds in Germany!—usually too short, with very long pillows. At HANNOVER we went to the *Hotel de Russie*, close to the station, and next morning continued our journey, *via* EISLEBEN, the birthplace of Luther, and HALLE, the birthplace of Händel, BRUNSWICK, where we drank some refreshing native stout, and MAGDEBOURG, where we dined and enjoyed excellent cooking.

CHAPTER IV.

DESCRIPTION OF DRESDEN

"DRESDEN, capital of the Kingdom of Saxony, head-"quarters of an army corps, and a favourite residence of "English people, styled the 'German Florence,' cele-"brated for cheap living, cheap good music, and works of art," so says *Bradshaw*, and doubtless this description is a true one. The autumn is not a good time of year at which to visit any Northern town if one would wish to experience an agreeable first impression, and towards the end of the month of October, 1888, cold and dreary weather had set in and the prospect was generally gloomy. I never anywhere experienced such a changeable climate; not much rain, dry in fact, scarcely any sunshine, cutting winds, heavy atmosphere, and sudden changes from frost to muggy weather and back again to frost; such is what one who winters in DRESDEN may expect to find. The opera house is a superb building, and comfortable inside. Performances take place five times a week, beginning at 6.30 or 7 o'clock. Prices are not high, the most expensive seats cost but 5s. 6d. and admission can be obtained by paying as little as 1s. The orchestra is first-rate, and figures in other capacities, for on Sunday it plays at the Hofkirche, where the masses of *Haydn, Mozart, Weber, Schubert, Hummel, Naumann, Reissiger*, and others are given with fine effect; and there are occasional concerts given at a hall called the *Gewerbehaus* where the same orchestra plays the symphonies of *Beethoven*, &c. There are also frequent concerts during the winter months at this *Gewerbehaus*, given by a different set of musicians, where you can go and enjoy the sweet sounds of the stringed instruments whilst quaffing the celebrated ales for which MUNICH has acquired such a high reputation. But what I found most enjoyable were the *Café restaurants* where musicians from different countries assemble and delight musical souls with their characteristic melodies. I mention the principal: The *Victoria salon*, almost opposite the Victoria Hotel in the *Waisenhaus strasse*, this is what in England would be called a "Variety Entertainment;" acrobats and conjurors perform here, but I heard a Swedish ladies' sextett who sang exquisitely. Then in the same street, right opposite the Victoria Hotel, is the *Welt restaurant*, an old-fashioned sort of a place, where a large orchestrion plays throughout the day and the visitor may dine for 6d., 9d., 1s., or 1s. 6d., and the food appears good, and the service clean. At this restaurant Tyrolese singers in costume play the zither and *jödel* away and afford much pleasure to their listeners. Next there is the *Café Tivoli* in the *Wettiner strasse*, some distance from the last two. At this place I heard a band of Hungarians in peasant costume. Then there is the *Pirnaischer Platz Café* at the end of the *König Johann strasse*, the newest and best street in DRESDEN, where I heard a band of Hungarian gipsies, in Hussar uniform, and a Servian octett, who played upon guitars, some of which were very diminutive. These guitars are manufactured at SZABADKA in Hungary. At this *café* as also at the *Welt* occasional afternoon performances are given, when smoking is prohibited. At the *Café Belvidere*, on the *Brühl Terrace*, overlooking the *Elbe*, there performs on the afternoons of Sundays and holidays a fine military band, and various restaurants and beer saloons will afford the visitor music of an evening. In the English and American quarter, across the railway from the principal part of the town, are situated the Russian, American, and Scotch churches. The American church is beautifully fitted up, and the singing is good there. The English church is over the railway, which must be reached by crossing the line. This is a great nuisance! as it is very tiresome to have to stand with a keen wind blowing, waiting until a train shall have passed. I cannot see the reason for not building a bridge or making an underground passage. The English church is too small for the number of visitors who flock to DRESDEN for the winter months. The pews are let out, and are mostly appropriated before the winter sets in, and it is next to impossible for a stranger to obtain a seat. Of the hotels the *Bellevue* has the best situation; it overlooks the river, is within a stone's throw of the opera house, two minutes' walk of the *Hofkirche*, and three minutes' walk from the picture gallery. The *Grand Union*, close opposite the railway station *(Altstadt)*, is an exceedingly comfortable house, and the cooking is excellent, but it labours under the disadvantage of being on the wrong side of the railway from the principal parts of the town, and the aforesaid nuisance of having frequently to wait while trains are passing and shunting is very much felt. In fact, this English and American quarter has advantages and disadvantages. It is close to the country, and one can get away to RACKNITZ and see the monument to *Moreau*, a Russian general with a French name, who was killed in battle in the year 1813, whilst fighting against the French, who were at that time in occupation of DRESDEN. From this spot there is a good view of the city and the hills across the *Elbe*, and also some of the hills belonging to *Saxon Switzerland* may be sighted. Then this part of the town is considered to be the most healthy, but it is a great drawback to be so far from the places of interest, with which DRESDEN abounds, and I should say that a more convenient quarter for visitors to stay at is to be found across the railway in the vicinity of the English church.

However, rents are higher in that part and living consequently more expensive. *Pensions* abound; in some streets nearly all the houses are boarding establishments or furnished apartments.

An account of the way of living at a *pension* may be interesting. The breakfasts, like all such meals in *Continental Europe*, exist principally in name. The boiled eggs which slip about like quicksilver and the poached ones which are served without toast, and are about as easy to eat with knife and fork as soup would be, are familiar to everyone. Germans don't breakfast, they merely drink a cup of coffee and eat a scrap of bread. One o'clock is the usual dinner hour. This consists of soup, seldom so good as English, but usually better than French, one or more kinds of hot meat, such as roast pork and boiled beef (with no salt in it), or roast beef and venison, which is good, and not eaten in that putrid condition which English people are so fond of, or roast veal and boiled pork, or roast mutton and poultry, also hare. Germans never eat rabbits, and hares come to table without their heads, which is less ghastly than the English fashion of retaining them. I found the mutton and beef much better than I had expected, but the pork is never done with the crackling on the top which we are so fond of in *England*. The meats are cut up and handed round, mixed up together on the same plate. Then follows some kind of pudding, usually good. The vegetables are potatoes, boiled and fried, *sauerkraut*, small carrots, turnips (not so well flavoured as English ones), pickled cabbage, &c. At seven "supper" as they call it takes place. This is generally cold with the exception of some weak tea and sometimes potatoes, and they also eat salad and cheese at this meal, which are things I don't relish with tea; and there is fruit of some kind, usually preserved, which I forgot to mention as being handed round at dinner with the meat. The cold meats consist of ham, cooked and raw, *paté* of pigs liver, pork cured in several ways, and anything that may have made its appearance hot at the dinner table the previous day. There are also sausages of various kinds, but these are usually sour and not much to the taste of an Englishman's palate. The Germans are immensely fond of the flesh of swine, and one frequently sees in the *Dresdener Anzeiger*, a daily paper which gives a list of all the different amusements, advertisements that *well-fleisch* is to be had at certain restaurants, that is to say a pig will be killed on a certain morning and the flesh will be boiled and eaten the same day. But I much prefer roast to boiled pork, particularly a nice juicy leg with crackling on the top. There are said not to be many Jews in DRESDEN, so the pork-butchers have a good time of it, although when staying at WIESBADEN, and ascertaining that there were two synagogues in that town, upon enquiring the reason, I was informed that there were two sets of Jews, the strict, who would not touch the flesh of pigs, and others, less strict, who would tuck into FRANKFORT sausages with as much delight as any patriotic sons of the *Fatherland*. The pork shops are most tastefully arranged, and one is never shocked by those disgusting sights which are so frequently to be met with in similar establishments in *England*. The sausages are of various sizes. Some more than three feet in length. A remarkable feature in *Germany* is the total absence of beggars. Those who have visited *Spain*, *Portugal*, *Italy*, or even *France* know what a deal of trouble the traveller has to put up with from this class, whilst those who have been to ROTTERDAM and the HAGUE have probably, like the writer, hurried away from those places, being fairly put to flight by the importunities of the guides who hover about the hotel doors and street corners and pounce upon the unlucky tourist whenever he shows his face. These men hang about many of the streets and squares of DRESDEN, but never on any account accost you after the manner of the confraternity in *Holland*. As the Germans possess such capacity for order and good management I am surprised that no rule of the road exists for foot passengers. On bridges across rivers you are obliged to keep on the right hand side, but elsewhere no rule exists and the shuffling to get out of people's way that takes place is very tiresome. Another inconvenience in DRESDEN is caused by the burning of coal, a brown kind from BOHEMIA; the consequence being that smuts fly about and play as much havoc with the faces of passers-by as they do in LONDON. The chimney sweeps usually wear the tall hat; this hideous contrivance is not much resorted to by other members of the community. In winter the inhabitants amuse themselves with skating. Numerous places are flooded over in different parts of the town, and at many of them bands of music are stationed. In the fine *Grosses-garten*, which corresponds to the *Hyde Park* of LONDON and *Bois de Boulogne* of PARIS, there are two good-sized sheets of water devoted to this purpose. The town at this time of year swarms with young English and American ladies. They come for the purpose of studying painting, music, and languages. Tuition is cheap as well as good, so DRESDEN has become about the most educational place in *Europe* so far as the fair sex is concerned.

CHAPTER V.

LEIPZIG.

IN the month of February, a party of five of us went to LEIPZIG. We put up at the hotel *Prussicherhof*, a large building in a good situation, but the *cuisine* being German we did not fare very well, and the charges were high for *Germany*. We had come to LEIPZIG far the purpose of attending a *Gewandhaus* concert which have the reputation of being the best classical concerts in *Germany*. The programme the evening we went was an excellent one—it included some exquisite music by *Gade*, the Norwegian composer for vocal quartette and orchestra, the *soprano* part being taken by *Frau Baumann*, whose voice was a perpetual flow of loveliness. The concert concluded with *Schuberts*' stupendous symphony in *C Major*, his last, formerly known as *No. 9*, but now, according to the opinion of that great critic, *Sir George Grove*, *No. 10*. I do not know any orchestral music grander than this symphony—it is the musical autobiography of a great genius. I was curious to see whether this LEIPZIG orchestra was in any way superior to the renowned *Crystal Palace* orchestra of *Mr. Manns*, but owing to the position of our seats it was impossible to form an opinion. All seats at these concerts being taken from season to season, strangers can only obtain any that the owners may not require for a particular evening. Ours were close underneath the orchestra and consequently much too near the music to hear it to perfection. The best plan at these concerts is to go to the morning rehearsal, a few days before the evening performance, when all seats are free. This I used to do at DRESDEN. The concert-room at LEIPZIG is magnificent, the music is divided into two parts, and between them the audience, as at an opera, promenades in a large corridor. I saw but few pretty faces in all that large assemblage. The *Saxons* certainly have no good looks to boast of as a rule. A delightful resort in LEIPZIG is *Auerbach's keller*, closely connected with the history of *Faust* and much frequented by *Goethe*. Here we enjoyed quite an English luncheon—ox-tail soup and *Barclay's* stout, both of which were excellent. There is a fine collection of pictures in LEIPZIG—we had been told that after the DRESDEN gallery it was not worth going to see, but we were very glad we had taken no notice of this advice. I find in travelling it is best to be cautious about taking the advice offered, there is so much jealousy between the inhabitants of one town and another. This LEIPZIG picture gallery has one advantage over that of DRESDEN and that is that you are able to get a better view of *all* the pictures. At DRESDEN some of them are hung so high up that it strains your neck to look at them, whilst at LEIPZIG there are only two "stories" as it were. We saw the new monument which had been unveiled the preceding autumn by the Emperor, but this was placed too near one end of a square to show to advantage.

I found the Royal Library in DRESDEN, across the river in the *Neustadt* a very convenient place to go to. It is open to the public free daily, after the manner of our *British Museum* reading-room, only no ticket of admission is required and it is quite a small affair. Having heard so much about *Saxon Switzerland*, I one morning took train to SCHANDAU, passing some fine river scenery, especially about KONIGSTEIN and the BASTEI rock. I travelled in a third class carriage and found it devoid of any cushion and comfortless. The snow was beginning to melt and the roads were slushy. We had had some very severe weather; on the 28th February, at 8.30 a.m. my thermometer stood at 12° *Fahrenheit* outside my window; but the houses are so comfortably warmed by means of porcelain stoves that one cannot be cold as in *England*, where it is sometimes colder in than out; and then the Germans have double windows which keep out both the cold in winter and heat in summer. I was called hurriedly away at the middle of March, and travelled without a break as far as LONDON. Leaving DRESDEN on the evening of the 13th, I arrived at BRUSSELS on the afternoon of the next day and proceeded late the same evening to CALAIS, crossed the Channel in the night, experiencing a cold but not rough passage in one of the old boats, and arrived in LONDON at six o'clock the following morning.

GENERAL VIEW OF AMBLESIDE.

CHAPTER VI.

AMBLESIDE.

THE month of May was remarkable in the English Lake District as being charmingly fine, brilliantly sunny and summer-like. Occasional thunder-storms helped to cool the air and prevent its becoming too oppressive. I stayed four weeks at *Compston House*, AMBLESIDE, opposite the old cricket-field and very near the church. This, I must say, I found to be the most comfortable lodging-house I had ever been to. It is kept by *Miss Irving*, and her cooking is everything that could be desired. It is unnecessary to say much about such a well-known place as AMBLESIDE; just little notices of comfortable quarters, however, may always be of use. The scenery looked as beautiful as could be possible, and as the summer rush of tourists had not set in the place generally was more enjoyable than during the season. It is a mistake to go to the Lakes during the months of July and August, although, of course, these are the only spare months that many people have. A great deal of rain is likely to fall in these months and when it doesn't and the weather is warm it is usually accompanied by heavy mists and damp heat which is very unhealthy.

CHAPTER VII.

SEASCALE.

FROM the beginning of June to the end of July we took a lodging-house at SEASCALE, a seaside resort on the *Cumberland* coast, now much frequented by people from the the South of *England*, and the same delightful weather we had experienced at AMBLESIDE obliged us with its presence at SEASCALE. This as a safe bathing place and affording fine sands for children is not surpassed by any I know. There are ten bathing-machines, small-sized things, drawn by a pony, but in calm weather it is pleasanter to bathe from the shore. A lot of fishing takes place, and salmon can be bought for as little as 10d. a pound during a great part of the season. There is a comfortable hotel at the station which has the advantage of being on the main line between WHITEHAVEN and LONDON, through carriages being run between those places every day during the summer. Then three very nice excursions can be made which are missed by those tourists who confine themselves to the beaten track. CALDER ABBEY some five miles distant, WASTWATER Lake, the most grand and gloomy in the district, which is only about seven miles off, and DALEGARTH Waterfall, sometimes called STANLEY GHYLL. But beware of SEASCALE in the month of August. The prices asked and received for lodgings then are enormous. They say that wealthy people from LIVERPOOL and MANCHESTER swarm at that time; so at the end of July a great exodus takes place; people with moderate means betake themselves off to make way for these long-pursed individuals.

RYDAL MOUNT, AS IT IS.

CHAPTER VIII.

SHAP WELLS, SILLOTH, AND GILSLAND.

IN August I made a little tour to SHAP WELLS, just off the railway line between TEBAY and PENRITH, which is noted for its steep ascent; I had visited this place in the summer of 1880, when I had stayed a fortnight and enjoyed it very much. This time we were bothered with wet weather. The hotel was rather over-crowded, and as the carving was all done by the guests it was a great nuisance. The table was very narrow and covered with such useless things as flowers, as well as all the meats and vegetables, and what with so many people being crowded together in a room with a low ceiling we were in a state of unpleasant perspiration during our meals. The mountain air of SHAP is very bracing, and two good excursions can be made in the neighbourhood, viz.: to HAWESWATER, a lake about fourteen miles off, seldom visited by tourists, being un-get-at-able from the Lake District, and to CROSBY-RAVENSWORTH, at a shorter distance away. The frequenters of this spa drink a great deal of the water, which is sulphureous and very disagreeable to the taste. It is, however, very efficacious, and many people who come to SHAP crippled with rheumatism are, after a short stay, enabled to walk with ease. After a few days' stay I went on to SILLOTH, a bathing-place on the SOLWAY, not far from CARLISLE. At the *Queen's Hotel* I found tolerable comfort, but the weather continued to be unsettled. The bathing at this place is not good; the water at low-tide recedes a great distance and leaves behind a muddy kind of sand, and there is no proper bathing accommodation for members of the sterner sex. There are also wanting some steps from the green down to the shore. SILLOTH is something of a shipping place. I returned to CARLISLE, and after spending a night at the comfortable *County Hotel* there, took train to GILSLAND, another mineral watering-place on the line to NEWCASTLE. They have a very fine hotel at GILSLAND called the *Shaws*, the visitors at which are divided into three classes. (There were two classes at SHAP.) After spending a few hours and partaking of a cold sulphur bath and luncheon I left the place.

CHAPTER IX.

NORTH EAST COAST OF BRITAIN.

ON 31st August we visited EDINBURGH and put up at the *Royal Hotel*, finely situated in *Prince's Street*, opposite the *Scott* monument. This hotel we did not like. The manageress and servants generally were extremely civil, but the house was too crowded for comfort, and our rooms looked out on to a back-yard, while a disagreeable smell of cooking pervaded them. The food was nastily cooked, and the charges were the highest. On the Sunday morning we attended service in *St. Giles'* Cathedral, and in the evening went to *St. Mary's*. We visited PORTOBELLO, a dreary seaside place; the new *Forth Bridge*, whither we drove in a public *char-a-banc*; HOLLYROOD, the castle, and a naval and military exhibition of pictures and weapons; I also took a walk up *Calton Hill*. I was glad to get away from EDINBURGH, which although a beautiful city, being uncomfortably quartered, I could not enjoy properly, and we spent a night at NORTH BERWICK, a seaside resort not far off, principally famous as a links where *golf* is played. We could not obtain accommodation in the *Marine* Hotel on the sea front, so went to the *Royal* at the station. I can't say much for this hotel, except that the people were very civil and charged us moderately. I was very disappointed with the food in *Scotland*. The *scones* were nasty things, the *whiskey* I did not like, and the *oatcake* was hard. Whilst in EDINBURGH I ordered a *Haggis*, which nearly made me sick. This took some time to prepare, as notice had to be given the previous day, and when it came to the table it was a great thing in a skin, and when I cut it my wife declares it gave a sort of bang and sent forth a most disagreeable smell. We very soon wearied of NORTH BERWICK and pushed on to BERWICK-ON-TWEED, stopping to see DUNBAR on the way. DUNBAR is principally a fishing town. We visited the ruins of the old castle and continued our journey to BERWICK. This border town charmed me greatly. It is situated on the north side of the river *Tweed*, whilst the town on the south side is called TWEEDMOUTH. Some people say that BERWICK is in *Scotland*, and so it ought to be, as it is the capital of BERWICKSHIRE;

others say that it is neither English nor Scotch, whilst a third set affirm that it is in England, and give as a reason, a pretty convincing one, that public-houses, which are closed all Sundays in *Scotland*, are open between church hours at BERWICK-ON-TWEED. Across the mouth of the river, which can be crossed by bridge or reached by ferry-steamer, lies SPITTAL, a sandy bathing-place, but there are no bathing-machines nor even tents, such as we saw at NORTH BERWICK. I tasted the water of an iron spring which was refreshing. I found the climate of BERWICK most exhilarating, and should have liked to delay there sometime.

The *King's Arms* hotel, an old-fashioned house was most snug, just the place to find comfort without unnecessary display. Modern hotels are more to be recommended for handsome furniture and ornamentation than for good living. One thing observable here was that *Coffee Room* was the name given to what in *Scotland* we had found termed *Dining Room*. Surely the latter is a much more suitable title for the room. After a night at BERWICK we went on to NEWCASTLE. We travelled after dark and so missed much that was, doubtless, well worth seeing. After resting for a night at the *County* Hotel, close opposite the railway station at NEWCASTLE, we went on to TYNEMOUTH and took up our abode for two days at the *Grand* Hotel, splendidly situated opposite the bathing-place. Just in front of the hotel stands a tremendous construction, built for an aquarium, which cost upwards of £80,000, and which we were told was to be sold for £15,000. This hotel possessed as fine a drawing-room as ever I came across—it was large and airy; the landlord very attentive, and the charges not dear considering the style of place. There was, however, one peculiarity, and that was the diminutive pieces of soap, and that of a hard quality which would not lather; everything else was plentiful, why was this? On the Sunday that we were at TYNEMOUTH the ferry brought shoals of people from SOUTH SHIELDS, which lies just across the mouth of the *Tyne*, whilst the town adjoining TYNEMOUTH on the north side is called NORTH SHIELDS. There is a mineral spring on the sands near the bathing-place, but the water is more tasteless than that at SPITTAL. At CULLERCOATS, half-a-mile on the cliff, is a very large church with good musical service. The organist played the most enchanting voluntary, and delightful little touches of music at intervals during the service. Whilst walking along the beach I found an old woman drying *seaweed*. She informed me that it was used for food.

The bathing-machines at TYNEMOUTH are very spacious and the seats broad and cushioned, an unusual thing—I never saw the like before. The water is clear, but ladies and gentlemen are not allowed to bathe together, which must be a great inconvenience to families. From TYNE-MOUTH to DURHAM is but a short journey—we pass through NEWCASTLE, from which an express takes us to DURHAM in twenty minutes. We had to drive a considerable distance to our hotel, the *Three Tuns*, a house more than three hundred years old, and how cozy an old place we found it! What an excellent dinner they gave us in a small parlour! and we formed a sociable party of six, besides ourselves being an American lady and her daughter and an English gentleman and his wife. The next day we attended the ten o'clock service at the cathedral, but what dreary music there was! The choir sang the anthem *Hear my Prayer* to a dismal tune by *Purcell*. Why, if they were incapable of rendering *Mendelssohn's* sublime music to these words, could they not sing the beautiful little piece of music which *Kent* has arranged to them? We afterwards visited the castle used as the university. The judge also on assize duty puts up here, and so does the Bishop occasionally. From DURHAM, the journey was by DARLINGTON over *Yorkshire* Moors to KIRKBY-STEPHEN in *Westmoreland*, a fine route; at one time we were over 1,700 feet above sea level. From OXENHOLME we traverse a picturesque line over parts of *Morecombe Bay*.

CHAPTER X.

JOURNEY TO PARIS.

AFTER spending a few days at that most magnificent and comfortable though very expensive hotel, the *Savoy*, on the *Victoria* Embankment, I left *Charing Cross* for FOLKESTONE and PARIS. We were a party of seven in all, counting two small children. The passage was pretty rough and we were one hour and fifty minutes in crossing. Owing to the PARIS Exhibition the crush on the boat and at BOULOGNE was very unpleasant and as usual, at the latter place, there were not enough railway carriages, and we had to sit eight grown up people and two children in a carriage intended to hold but eight. How uncomfortable railway travelling in *France* is! especially on the Northern line—small carriages and never enough of them; all clamour and confusion, blowing of horns as if embarking on a hunting expedition, hurry and scurry, not enough time allowed to eat a meal without a subsequent attack of indigestion, and on most lines nothing but first-class carriages to express trains, and no means of warming them in cold weather—nothing but those foot-pans with which we are so familiar in *England*, as if keeping one's toes warm made up for suffering cold in other parts of the body. I think the French are more backward as regards comfort in railway travel than any other people I have been amongst with the exception perhaps of the Portuguese. And whilst on this topic I will add a few further remarks :—Although railway travelling was first instituted in *England*, and our trains go at a greater speed than those in other countries, still the Germans have brought this mode of locomotion to a greater degree of perfection. Their second class carriages are, as a rule, superior to those in *England*. You frequently find lavatories attached to them, to enjoy which commodities you are bound to travel first class in *England*. In winter the carriages are warmed, aud one is able by pulling a plug to regulate the temperature. We know not this luxury in *England*. But the one thing which makes *England* far behind the whole continent (including even *France* and *Portugal*) is the system, or more properly speaking want of system, about luggage. After your things have been deposited in the luggage van you know not whether you will ever see them again. When you arrive at your destination you make a rush for the luggage van and point and shout "that's mine, that's mine," and no matter if you were to claim the whole contents of the van, the porter would consider it all to be your property; now, what can be easier than for a thief to say "that's mine," pointing to the box belonging to some old lady before she has had time to "alight" from her carriage, to adopt an expression much used by guards. And should she discover the thief walking off with her property, he merely says he is "very sorry, he mistook it for his own," and there the matter ends; he runs no risk, he has all to gain, nothing to lose by attempting a robbery. If you go from LONDON to BRIGHTON your luggage *is* registered—but that is quite an exception as far as my experience goes. But we are arrived at BOULOGNE, a delightful place to sojourn at during the bathing season, but a most inconvenient place to have to pass hurriedly through. And now whom are to blame for all this inconvenience occasioned to travellers? Were it not for the obstinacy of some English people, by this time there would be a tunnel underneath the channel and we should be able to take our seats at *Charing Cross* or *Victoria* and be troubled no more until our arrival in PARIS. This matter, however, will never be decided by merely taking into consideration the convenience of tourists, it is from the commercial point of view that it must principally be regarded, but not being a commercial man I am unable to treat of the subject from that standpoint. The military objection I regard as nonsensical, and look forward to the time, not I trust very far distant, when the mass of English people will rise above insular prejudice and give their votes in favour of this scheme for facilitating intercommunication betwixt the greatest of naval powers and the, until recently generally recognised leader of the military powers of *Europe*. There is reason to hope for a speedy termination of this absurd opposition. *Mr. Gladstone* has given his sanction to the scheme, and let us hope that after he has settled the hitherto seemingly interminable Irish question by granting to the Irish their now very reasonable demands, which all experience is in favour of his doing, let us hope that he will devote what energy may be left to his apparently exhaustless frame to the advocating of a mighty scientific project which according to *Sir Edward Watkin* its principal promoter, would tend to knit together two of the leading nations of *Europe* in closer friendship.

Avaunt ye bull-headed fanatics, reared in the foggy atmosphere of the cockney metropolis! Avaunt ye scaremongers suspicious of treason at every turn! Avaunt ye military martinets let your foolish utterances no more be heard against the construction of a tunnel between *France* and *England* !

CHAPTER XI.

FROM PARIS TO WIEN.

ON arriving at PARIS, owing, I suppose, to the great number of passengers, no boxes were opened, and we drove to the *Hôtel Terminus*, close by the *St. Lazare* railway station, a new hotel only opened at the same time as the exhibition, a fine building, but I did not think much of the food, and the waiters were not a very polite lot. The following day (October 6th) *335,000* persons attended the exhibition. At the exhibition, attracted by the strains of violins, we entered a restaurant and found a band of Hungarians, dressed in scarlet, performing their wild, woodland music as well as some of the popular dances of the day. This band was about the best I ever heard. These gipsies have a knack of bringing forth the sweetest tones from their violins which even such performers as *Herr Joachim* and *Madame Neruda* do not possess.

The next day, after seeing the rest of the party off *en route* to *Portugal* from the *Orleans* station where there was a great crowd of French and Spaniards returning South, I took steamer to the exhibition and made another inspection of it. The pictures were very fine. I jumped into a train, and after imagining that I had been taken right outside the grounds discovered that I had merely been transported to another part of them—so vast a place was it.

I took a ride on the new hydraulic railway, which it is said will go one hundred miles or more an hour, but we were taken such a short distance that no great speed was attained and I was able to form no opinion on the subject. There was such crowding and confusion at PARIS that I was glad to drive to the *Bâle* station and depart for *Austria*. At this station there was a greater crush than ever. Swiss and Austrians were returning to their respective countries. On arriving at the Swiss frontier no luggage was looked at and we changed at BASEL for ZURICH, where I had again to change and yet again at BUCHS; at this latter place both my traps were opened, the Austrians being very particular in this respect. I never before had seen *Switzerland* looking so beau-

INNSBRUCK.

MERAN.

tiful, the colouring was glorious, especially about the lower end of ZURICH lake. We were seventeen minutes I believe in the ARLBERG tunnel, and arrived at INNSBRUCK in the evening. I put up at the *Tirolerhof*, where I had stayed on a former occasion; it is a most comfortable house, but expensive for *Tirol*. The river looked bewitching by moonlight. The following day there was, as usual, a regular hurricane (I never knew such a windy place as INNSBRUCK), so before my turn came to be swept completely away by the boisterous element I left for MERAN, crossing the sublimely grand *Brenner Pass*, and reached my destination shortly before nine. The *Habsburgherhof* is a charming hotel and the charges are so moderate. I am sure the *Cuisine* could not be beaten anywhere, and for dinner we were charged but 2s. 6d. and for supper 1s. 8d. The climate was mild ; there was a total absence of sun and some very heavy rain. The place is very lovely, but I should say dull to spend much time at. The river *Passer* was very much swollen and dashed at furious speed through the town ; and the following morning when I left for SALZBURG the railway line was at parts under water, and all along the river's banks for many a mile were people stationed with long poles with hooks at the ends of them trying to catch the floating timber or anything else that might be swept by. Upon re-crossing the *Brenner* we were detained by an avalanche. There had been a fall of snow up on the mountains and the heavy rains had washed it down with such force that trees had been uprooted and scattered over the railway track. From INNSBRUCK to SALZBURG the rocking of the train was most disagreeable. It was half-past midnight when I entered the *hotel de l'Europe*, close by SALZBURG railway station, and demanded accommodation for the night. What comfort was here ! I had electric light in my room, an electric lamp by my bedside. I drank *Vöslauer* and *Erlauer* of the very best quality, and fed upon the best of food. In the morning I was up betimes, for it was Sunday and I wished to attend High Mass at the cathedral, after which I paid a visit to *Mozart's* birthplace and found there the same old caretaker I had encountered on former occasions. There was a haze over the city so that I could not appreciate its beauties. In the evening I went and supped at the *Cursalon* where a military band played the most enthralling music, and left the capital of the SALZKAMMERGUT at halfpast twelve at night or rather early morning and had a fatiguing six hours or more journey to WIEN.* I was only

---

* VIENNA, as it is best known in *England*, but I see no reason in calling a *German* city by an *Italian* name.

just in time in re-crossing the *Brenner* as the very day I arrived in WIEN the Emperor was to have gone to MERAN to join his wife and daughter, but was prevented by the floods.

WIEN is a city that one hears of as being situated on the "Beautiful Blue Danube," but this is a double mistake. It is two miles from the centre of the city to the river, which I have never yet seen anywhere of anything approaching to a bluish colour. A canal has been made to connect the river with the town, and strangers might at first sight take this to be the Danube itself. It is a vilely-paved place, so much so that there is no pleasure in walking through its streets, and the noise of the traffic is deafening. The principal street, the *Ring strasse*, which encircles the principal part of the city, is good for traffic, but not much better than the rest of WIEN for foot passengers. It also possesses the reputation of being a place for good living—I have not found it so. The Austrians are wretched cooks, and unless you manage to find a French restaurant you run the chance of faring very badly. At the Hotel *Muller*, at the end of the *Graben*, and also at the *Continental* Hotel, across the canal, you can enjoy good cooking. At the Imperial Palace I saw an Hungarian guard relieve a *Jäger* one. The bands played very inspiriting airs. I visited, one evening, *Ronacher's*, a large music hall, all gilding and ornamentation, which was crowded with people, eating, drinking, and smoking. The entertainment was a variety one, and two Englishmen were acting as buffoons and trying their hands, or more correctly speaking their tongues, at the German and French languages, but they soon were obliged to express themselves in their own language. I also went to the *Café Lyra;* a *damen-kapelle*, and a *Herren-kapelle* perform at this place. The men violinists played the *Rakóczy* march with such spirit and animation that I can truly say I never heard so fine a performance. The prettiest building in WIEN to my idea is the spire of *St. Stephen's*, but what is really more striking than anything else is the elegance of the girls and women—they possess the finest figures I have ever seen, and go along in quite a military manner.

SALZBURG.

CHAPTER XII.

BUDAPEST.

AFTER two days' stay in the *Kaiserstadt*, I left for BUDAPEST, a journey of less than six hours by train. The route lay by RAAB and KOMORN, at which latter place the river *Waag* joins the Danube, and there is said to

ST. STEPHEN'S CATHEDRAL, WIEN.

be good scenery, but it was too dark for a view. On a former occasion I had gone the other way, by PRESBURG, it was summer time, and I shall never forget my first hearing of a gipsy band—it was at the station of NEUHAUSL, some twenty-five or thirty miles across the Hungarian frontier. There stood about half-a-dozen merry-looking little fellows all fiddling away and appearing to be so pleased with themselves! and upon my return from PEST a few days afterwards there they were, the same little men still at it! There is some fine river scenery at VISSEGRAD, between GRAN and BUDAPEST, but nothing much else I believe until that most beautifully-situated of all the European capitals itself is reached. I can never understand the mysterious manner in which one always approaches PEST. We seem to cross and re-cross the giant Danube. We get glimpses of lights shining brilliantly as if a grand illumination had been organised to welcome us to this fairy-like "City of the Magyar." Then we lose sight of all this and begin to think we have been deceived, that we have had as it were a sort of foretaste of *Paradise*, but are now being speeded away from all this loveliness to drag along the stale dismal routine of our earthly existence. It is too tantalizing by far. Again we see those lights reflected in the swift waters of the mighty river, again the same kind of disappointment is experienced until at last after much shrill screaming from "Puffing Billy" (I know not the Hungarian name for this gentleman), we enter the finely-built station of the *Austro-Hungarian* States railway.

At BUDAPEST an examination of luggage takes place; this custom prevails in many Continental towns, and it is a great nuisance. Nothing is allowed to be brought into the towns to be sold, all such things as poultry and eggs, etc. being taxed; it is hard on the peasantry, and makes residence in towns, as far as food is concerned, more expensive than in *England*. However, on this occasion they opened nothing belonging to me, and I sallied forth to find a conveyance to take me and mine to the *Grand hotel Hungaria,—Nagy szalloda Hungaria* in Magyar *parlance*. Now, well-knowing the extravagant prices one has to pay in PEST for cabs,* methought to do the economical, and espying an omnibus that had something on it that I took to mean *Grand Hotel Hungaria*, I hailed the conductor, and after taking my seat was driven at

---

* A noticeable thing in both WIEN and PEST is the scarcity of one-horsed carriages. You are thus on arriving at a railway station obliged to hire a two-horsed machine, and they make you pay at the rate of 2/6 or 3/- a mile, more than double what you are charged in LONDON for a one-horsed trap.

a rapid pace through the city. But I soon discovered that this little bit of penny wisdom was likely to cost me dear in the end. I tendered the man a florin which he pocketed, never offering me any change, and it is my belief that had I given him a note of the value of one hundred florins he would have put it into his pocket as a matter of course, but we had not gone a very long distance when this rascal signalled to a *Träger* to come and take my luggage out of the onmibus, and I soon found myself together with my goods and chattels deposited in the middle of a street. It turned out that the omnibus did not go to the hotel at all, and this *Träger* had much difficulty in trudging along with my *impedimenta*. Arrived at the hotel in this uncereomonious fashion, my *Träger* behind me staggering under the weight of the packages, I find in the entrance hall a great array of persons (there seems to be an extra supply of everybody) all ready to bid me welcome to their splendid hostelry. It would be after ten o'clock when I find my way to the *Et Terem* (Hungarian for dining-room) where in one corner of the room are stationed some eight or ten swarthy little fellows all hard at work scraping away at their violins. The place is alive with merriment, waiters brush briskly by, people are chatting and laughing, aye, and smoking too, for smoking is allowed in the dining halls of almost all Austrian and Hungarian hotels.*

The following day I devoted to a visit to BUDA (pronounced *Booda*.) This, the older town of the two, lies across the Danube, and is reached by a fine suspension bridge,† which was erected forty years ago by *Mr. Tierney Clarke*, the architect of the *Hammersmith* bridge. Just over the bridge a lift takes you to the Royal Palace of the King of Hungary. The grounds are open to the public, and a fine view of PEST is obtained from them. Having descended I wander on through the badly paved streets of the Servian quarter where I pass many flaxen-haired children, and eventually reach the summit of the *Blocksberg*, from which I enjoy a fine view of the surrounding country and the twin cities lying below. Then I descend and visit the *Blocksbad*—a door is opened and I enter the public bath. Some old women in chemises call out for me to shut the door as they fear the effects of the air. The temperature seems to suffocate. I soak with per-

---

* At the *Schweitzer* in ORSOVA even the waiters smoked.

† A curious coincidence connected with this bridge is, that when they were working at it, remains were found of one that King *Matthias Corvinus* had attempted to set up.

spiration.‡ After this I pay visits to the *Bruckbad, Lukasbad,* and *Königsbad,* and not far from the latter approach a landing-stage in order to take steamer to the *Margit* Isle. Whilst waiting here I get into conversation in German with an old Hungarian from the *Carpathians,* who in the face was very like what *Deak,* the Hungarian patriot must have been, if the latter's pictures and statues do him justice. This old Hungarian informed me that being an Englishman I was of German origin. I don't know that he was right. We English are a mongrel race of people, and I daresay we are as much Danish or Norman as Saxon. Our conversation was interrupted by the arrival of the steamer, and in a few

VIEW FROM HOTEL HUNGARIA, BUDAPEST.

minutes I am landed on what in summer I have found to be an enjoyable resort, but which at this time of year presented a dreary appearance. I have difficulty in finding a restaurant open, at length I discover one and order some food. An energetic little waiter brings me soup—but where is the

---

‡ *M. Victor Tissot* in his *Unknown Hungary* says, that if you go to the *Blocksbad* at six o'clock on a Sunday morning in Summertime, you will find it full of beautiful peasant girls clad simply in nature's garb. *M. Tissot*, however, does not speak from personal experience, he merely relates what he has been told. For my part, having visited the *Blocksbad* three times, though not at the day or hour specified by *M. Tissot* I have found the women to be the veriest hags.

spoon to eat it with? Now it is a curious fact that I cannot say "spoon" in any language but English. This is, perhaps, owing to my not being of a "spoony" disposition. However, the waiter understands what I want and runs at great speed across the room to fetch that most necessary article with which he has forgotten to supply me. On an omelette making its appearance, again a spoon is wanting, and again the little waiter runs at full speed to get one. A steamer takes me back to PEST and lands me a few yards from the hotel. A few words about this hotel. It is now the only one with a river view. The *Europa*, where I stayed in 1883, has been closed and now the *Hungaria* is the only hotel in PEST overlooking the river. It is a very fine building and possesses what is very rare in this part of the world—a most comfortable public sitting-room. When I visited it, in 1882, such a room did not exist. There is a very commodious lift; a separate room for breakfast; and a salon with grand piano in it. The attendance is excellent; the cooking is A1. There is a large dining-room; but the most agreeable way is to take your meals in the large glass-covered court-yard, where little tables are placed here and there. Although I only saw some half-a-dozen English people I was told that there were forty staying in the hotel at the time, amongst them being a Church of England clergyman who on Sunday conducts service in the hotel.

CHAPTER XIII.

TOUR IN HUNGARY.

A JOURNEY of a little over three hours by rail brought me to the typical Hungarian town of SZEGED (*German Szegedin*), which in the year 1879 was almost totally destroyed by flood. Now an embankment has been made

SZEGED.

and a fine bridge erected across the river *Tisza* (*Theiss* in German) by the celebrated *M. Eiffel*. Having been recommended to do so I put up at the hotel *Tisza* opposite the opera house, and near to the river. I here discovered that the splendid band we had heard the previous week in PARIS belonged to SZEGED, so there was no gipsy music for me to enjoy. One drawback I found at the hotel, the sanitary arrangements were the worst I came across during the whole of this Austro-Hungarian tour. The following day being Sunday a large market was held in the gigantic square, the costumes were more picturesque than any I have ever seen elsewhere, red seeming to be the favourite colour. Many of the girls wore their hair in two plaits down their backs entwined with coloured ribbons, the effect of which was very pleasing. Past SZEGED we traverse the vast plain of the *Alföld*, a dreary expanse of land where now and again the eye rests on herds of cattle, droves of horses, flocks of sheep, pigs and geese, all carefully tended by men dressed in white petticoats, their hair flowing over their shoulders. I had as a companion for a short distance a Servian doctor who offered me some grapes and struck up a conversation, but we could hardly understand one another; after this, a pleasant Hungarian and an elderly man who spoke French. In the carriage were looking-glass and table. It was half-past nine when the dark mountains of Servia came in view, frowning in gloomy silence across the Danube. This is BAZIAS. A dark Jewish-looking woman shows me into a room over the *buffet* at the railway station, where I go for a few hours' repose, as the steamer *is timed* to start at five o'clock in the morning. I am up and dressed by four, and stumble along in the dark to the landing-stage, but it is nearly half-past eleven when the boat arrives. Many curiously-dressed Wallachs are about here. These people do most of the hard work. On the steamer, I have reason to believe I am the only tourist; there is an elderly military officer, but most of the passengers are evidently travelling on business. There are three classes, and this mode of travel is more expensive than going by rail. Soon we pass a Servian village, the only one until we get opposite to ORSOVA. The country all along the Servian side is beautifully wooded, but there is almost a dearth of inhabitants. On the Hungarian side there are several villages, and a well-made road follows the river's bank, and eventually leads into Roumania. The scenery about MOLDOVA and DRENKOVA is very fine, but, of course, the grandest sight this day was to be witnessed at the defile of *Kasan*, where the rocks are said to rise two thousand feet straight up out of the water on each side of the river. I was much struck with ORSOVA. The town, or rather I should say village, consists of two parallel streets of considerable length; along the river's bank is a boulevard from which there is a grand view across the water.

D

I noticed many sweet faces in ORSOVA, and drank some good Servian wine called *Negotiner Ausbruch*, a rich dark wine, but had to make the best of a most uncomfortable bed. The following morning was brilliant with sunshine. I made another examination of the place and entered a small church where some fine organ-playing was going on. After this I took a walk past Neu Orsova as far as VERCIOROVA, the frontier village of Roumania. NEU ORSOVA (in Turkish, ADAKALEH) is a fortified island on the Danube; it was founded by the Turks. Its appearance is most picturesque, in fact, I do not think I ever saw so beautiful an island; it has to be reached by boat. However, I did not go there, but continued along the high road. I passed a turbaned Turk

ADAKALEH OR NEW ORSOVA.

and some extraordinary looking beings, I could not make out what they were, they seemed to be nuns, but had quite a masculine appearance. One of them wished me "Good day," at least I suppose it meant so. I follow, for the roadway follows along the side of the railway, and when about four miles from ORSOVA enter Roumanian territory, I pass the guard-house unchallenged, and ramble on through the village. What peculiarly-dressed people are here! There is a Greek priest in his tall head-gear. I cannot describe what I saw: it would require an expert in the millinery art to do so. In the distance I hear the roar of the cataracts at the *Iron gates* and admire the shapes of the cliffs as they slope down to the water's edge. I retrace my steps and approach the Hungarian guard-house, when, lo! I am called upon to halt; and asked to produce my passport. Not possessing one I hand to the official the *Lettre d'Indication* I have received from my bank for the purpose of enabling me to cash my circular notes, but am told that this is no passport, and that I must turn back and stay in Roumania until I can procure one. This was a pretty pass to have come to! Myself in one country and my luggage and money in another. However, after some parleying I was allowed to re-enter Hungary. I have since pondered over in my mind the course I should have pursued had I been prohibited from returning to Hungary. I believe I might have broken over the mountains, but I think I should have taken the next train from VERCIOROVA to ORSOVA, the station at the latter place being only a mile or so from the village, whereas the frontier guardhouse was some four miles distant, and then they could have detained me at ORSOVA station until a messenger had been despatched to the hotel for my things; after this I should have had to go back to Roumania as far on as to BUCHAREST and procure a passport there. But supposing that after the Hungarians had refused to have me back the Roumanians had turned me back also, in that case I should have been sent backward and forward like a shuttlecock on a little piece of "no man's land" that lay between the two countries. However, here I am in "La Belle France" as the saying has it, writing my narrative in peace and comfort.*

As I re-passed ADAKALEH a chorus was wafted across the water from Servia, and presently I visited the *Kronkapelle*,† where the crown and regalia of Hungary are preserved.

Arrived at the inn I refreshed myself with some PANCSOVA beer, and in the afternoon left lovely ORSOVA for the baths of MEHADIA.‡ HERCULESBAD or HERCULES-FÜRDO station is only twelve miles from ORSOVA, but there is a drive of about two miles from it to the village. This place I had come to out of the season. I am a good hand at doing that: having visited many fashionable resorts and been almost the only stranger there. But one hotel was open, and that was the *Franzenhof;* it was a dreary, poorly-furnished house, and no food was to be got in it. Two restaurants

---

* Why "La Belle France!" As far as my experience goes there is little of the beautiful in that country. Certainly *Savoy* and *Piedmont* are lovely provinces, but they have been but recently acquired by *France*, and I take it the saying dates back prior to that event.

† A description of this place is given in a delightfully written book entitled "Magyarland," published by Messrs. Sampson, Low & Co.

‡ Two things are noticeable in Southern Hungary—the dirtiness of the salt and the badness of the butter.

were open across the street however, and in front of one sat the elderly officer whom I had seen on board the steamer the previous day, and entering I partook of my meal in close proximity to his servant, whose presence was not at all a benefit to me, as he kept up a constant spitting upon the floor, a disgusting habit which prevails wherever I have been on the Continent, and amongst all classes of the community. It is said to be attributable to the kind of cigarettes foreigners smoke.

The principal bathing-establishments at HERCULESBAD were closed for the winter, but I was recompensed for all this

KRONKAPELLE AT ORSOVA.

by the beauty of the scenery. I walked some distance up the valley of the *Czerna* down which the river was rushing at great speed, and was much reminded of Switzerland, only no watering-place in that country that I have ever seen possesses such grand scenery as that about MEHADIA. The weather was summerlike, and having walked myself into a perspiration, on my return to the hotel I thought to have a mineral bath, and was accordingly conducted to the *Ludwigsbad* and spent half-an-hour in the bath, which I afterwards found made me very drowsy, and I arrived late the same evening at TEMESVAR in a rather exhausted condition which was aggravated by a long drive from the station over badly-paved streets. However, when I reached the hotel *Kronprinz Rudolf* I was soon enabled to pull myself together again. It would be ten o'clock or later when I entered the dining-hall, which was divided by a narrow passage into two parts.

I will now make a few observations on the difference in the ways of living between the English and the Hungarians. Supposing you were to enter the dining-room of an hotel of an English provincial town, containing a population of some thirty thousand or forty thousand inhabitants, at so late an

CURSALON, MEHADIA.

hour as ten o'clock on an October night, what sort of a reception would you meet with? Why, you would find the gas lowered, and in a corner of the room you might descry a waiter either fast asleep or else nearly yawning off the top of his head. On your demanding a chop or steak you would be told that the kitchen was closed, and that all you could have to eat was cold meat and cheese. Now mark the difference here. In the passage, I have alluded to above, there is stationed a gipsy band—they have probably been there for two hours—(for these bands usually play from eight o'clock until midnight)—they have thoroughly warmed up to their work, and play with full fury. The halls are brilliant with electric light and thronged with people enjoying their musical supper, and amongst many other members of the profession of arms there sits the elderly officer whom I have seen on board the steamer and at the baths of MEHADIA. Upon my asking for a bill of fare, one nearly a yard long is brought to me. I soon "set to" and enjoy a capital supper, followed by a bottle of *Ruster Ausbruch*, a delicious *muscatel* wine, and having revelled for sometime in the rhapsodical strains of the weird wild music of the Hungarian gipsies, I retire to my couch a merrier and I trust a wiser man. The following day I walked about TEMESVAR. They have a fine park, and I also found myself on a Common, with soldiers drilling in every

TRINKGROTTE, CURSALON AND GISELLA PARK, MEHADIA.

direction. Here were some encampments of gipsies—the first I had come across in Hungary; it is a mistake to suppose that the gipsy musicians one hears in the large towns are the same class of people as those uncouth beings who roam about the country. They come of the same stock, but are thoroughly civilized. This day I had for luncheon an exquisite omelette, a species of the culinary art at which Hungarians excel. Their coffee too is the best I have ever tasted. When I got back to PEST, I found the same band in the dining-hall as I had heard performing on the first night of my arrival, and this being my last night in the Hungarian capital, I make a point of sitting up till midnight so as to hear the last of it all, but no, the gipsies don't go, and I leave them still fiddling away at that hour of the night when ghosts and sprites take their walks abroad. In the morning I paid a visit to the academy of pictures, and having some difficulty in finding the entrance, accosted a man who appeared to be a porter, and who addressed me as " My Lord " and nearly bowed himself down to the ground. Afterwards I wended my way to the national museum and picture gallery, at the portal of which stood a "Mighty man of valour," dressed in full hussar uniform, busby with shaving-brush on top, sword and all. His duty was merely to take charge of sticks and umbrellas. Display of uniform is observable throughout *Germany* and *Hungary*. In BUDAPEST the police have red and green ribbons round their hats, and swords by their sides. I once or twice saw the white tunic. Many women, in both WIEN and PEST, wear the *mantilla* after the manner of their sisters in *Spain* and *Italy*. I was rather surprised to learn that the Austrians are not taught the English language in their schools as the North Germans are; they pronounce, too, some words differently from the rest of the Teuton nationalities; for instance, *eu* is pronounced like *ei* and not as *oi* in other parts of *Germany*. The Hungarians apparently only learn the German language in addition to their own. The latter place their Christian names *after* their surnames. All the streets in BUDAPEST are labelled in Hungarian. A great many boys are employed as waiters in *Austria* and *Hungary*. If we cannot have women to wait upon us, who are really best adapted for the purpose, boys are preferable to men in my opinion. A very stupid custom is to charge extra for every piece of bread you may eat at a meal, even when you go in for a meal at a fixed price. How different from what obtains in *France*, where " pain à discretion " has become quite a saying. Another peculiarity about hotels in the Austrian Empire is that you have to pay ready money for everything you eat and drink, except what is served to you in your room. When you want your bill (which only includes the charge for your room, bath, attendance, etc.) you ring for the floor waiter, and he delivers it to you. At the *Hungaria* I was amused by the persistent way in which an Englishman kept importuning a waiter for his bill, not, of course, being up to the manners and customs of this somewhat peculiar country. With the exception of *Tirol*, SALZBURG, and TRIESTE, I have met with no *table d'hôte* meals in *Austria*. Fruit and cheese are always served in the same plate. In *Hungary* a tiny plate containing several kinds of vegetables is always placed before you. *Paprika*, a very red-coloured native pepper, but not as hot as *Cayenne*, is on every table in *Hungary*. Very good wines to drink are, in Austria, *Vöslauer*, and in Hungary, *Château Paliguay*, *Erlauer*, and *Kamenitzi* (the red, not the white); this latter is of a most generous quality, but you will not find it everywhere. Soup is very cheap all through these countries—the price usually varies from six to ten *kreutzers* a basin. Sometimes you may see a soup charged as much as twenty *kreutzers*, but very seldom. At the hotel *Europa*, at PEST, I have had delicious gravy soup for ten *kreutzers* (twopence in English money). Another advantage! the postage is cheaper than in any other country—you can send a post card all the way from ORSOVA to HAMBURGH for two *kreutzers* (less than a halfpenny), and stamps for letters to foreign countries cost but twopence each. The Exchange, when I was in *Austria-Hungary* this time was low. I only got 119 *gulden* for £10. I was informed that sometimes the Exchange was so high that 130 *gulden* were given for £10 English. In *France* and *Spain* too, I only got exactly 250 *francs* or *pesetas* for a £10 note. Nearly all their money in *Austria* is in paper, I only became possessed of about eight silver *gulden* during my twenty five days stay in this Empire, and several of those were given to me at my request. As for gold they have none. I found it the same in Spain—no gold, but silver pieces up to five *pesetas* in value. However, French gold goes in *Spain*, and English gold circulates abundantly in *Portugal*. Hungarian railway stations are very picturesque, so many shrubs and trees being planted about them. Railway travelling is cheap too. You can go fifteen-and-a-half miles first class for a shilling; second class for tenpence; and third class for sixpence—this is by express; it is even cheaper by slow trains. You can go 140 miles *and upwards*, that is to say, you *could go* 140,000 miles, should the line extend to such a distance (which of course it does not, as the kingdom of *Hungary* is *not* boundless), third class, for four *gulden*, that is six shillings and eightpence in English money, but these exceedingly low fares are only on the Hungarian State and Hungarian North-Eastern railways. I was not up to this dodge, as in a subsequent part of my journey I booked from ZAKANY only as far as AGRAM and again from AGRAM to FIUME, when I might have taken a ticket all the way from ZAKANY to FIUME for the same amount as what I paid for the one from AGRAM to FIUME.

CHAPTER XIV.

FROM PEST TO GÖRZ.

BUT. I am digressing. The hour has come for me to leave this adorable city—a little open one-horsed carriage draws up at the door of the hotel, and I am soon being driven over the grand bridge which spans the Danube. And oh! what a scene of glory bursts upon my view as I cross the river! The lights of BUDA in front and those of PEST behind extend for miles and are reflected in the deep waters below. Can I quit such a picture of delight? Can I tear myself away from so celestial a city? Alas! it must be so! Farewell thou guardian *Blocksberg*, bold defender of the capital of the fiery Magyar! Farewell ye shrivelled hags who lave your clay in the boiling baths of BUDA! Farewell ye gay and joyous *Czigánòk* who rejoice the heart of man with your intoxicating music! Farewell my blood-red *Kamenitzi*, nectar given to cheer the soul as it sojourns here below in corporeal confinement!

I am whisked away and arrive at KANIZSA after midnight, and having five hours to wait, seek rest for my wearied limbs, and the station master places a pillow on a seat in one of the waiting-rooms, and I lie down until four o'clock, at which hour the gas is turned on and there is much bustle, as a train from some quarter is expected. The journey to AGRAM is most uninteresting—a flat marshy country, and AGRAM itself is a stupid place; nothing of interest to be seen in it. The peasants I noticed used red umbrellas, and the women, many of whom were good-looking, wore very short dresses and top boots. It had been raining heavily and the town was in a filthy condition. There were also bad smells. At the hotel I stopped at, the *Kaiser von Oesterreich*, I have reason to believe that I got pretty well swindled all round, and I should advise nobody to go there—but I suppose scarcely anybody would think of going to such a place as AGRAM. None but commercial travellers about. Nothing worth seeing till we arrive at KARLSTADT, where the country assumes a picturesque appearance, which continues and expands to grandeur as we approach FIUME. What I ought to have done would be to have gone by express from PEST to FIUME and then from FIUME to KARLSTADT and back. All the journey from KANIZSA to KARLSTADT is so much waste; but of course I knew no better, and I hope that if any of my readers should ever contemplate a trip to these parts they will take my advice and give AGRAM a wide berth. After KARLSTADT we get on the *Karst*, that wild craggy region which extends for many miles about here. At FIUME I put up at the *Hotel Europa*, and there being a colonel staying in the house, the band of his regiment serenaded him and played some excellent

ABBAZIA.

music. This was so warm a climate that my thermometer registered 73 degrees *Fahrenheit* outside the window at ten o'clock at night—this was on the 28th October.

The next morning I left for ABBAZIA—a little steamer plies across the bay of *Quarnero*, and reaches this newly-created resort in fifty minutes. FIUME being a free port luggage is examined at ABBAZIA. The hotel *Stephanie* is an elegant building. I stayed there two wet days; it was so rainy that going out of doors was almost an impossibility, and there were very few people in the hotel, it being between the seasons. Living, too, was very expensive, and I went on to ADELSBERG, having an idea of visiting the newly-discovered grotto there. Allbeit, ABBAZIA is a beautiful place, as lovely a bay as ever I saw. A drive of some few miles brought me to the station of MATUGLIE, where I took train to ADELSBERG. I had previously visited this place and been shown through the extensive grotto which has brought it to notice. The spacious Swiss hotel (for the proprietor, *Herr Progler* is a native of *Helvetia*) stands on an elevated position in its own grounds. The following morning having signified my intention of exploring the newly-discovered cavern I am driven by omnibus to the spot, where we enter the old grotto; from this point it is necessary to walk, and accompanied by the porter of the hotel (an excitable Hungarian) I trudge along through the mud to a village, where we are met by an invalidish-looking man dressed in a suit of green with hat to match. He escorts us as we " tramp o'er moss and fell." We come across traces of a bear. We leap like nimble goats from rock to rock, till at length we succeed in reaching the mouth of the cavern, where we find a gate firmly locked, but some men being at work inside my two companions set up a great shouting, and some boys in the meantime having joined the party, add their voices to those of the porter and the man in green. Meanwhile, I wander about, and ascend in one direction and then in another. The porter begins talking; he is inquisitive as to where I have come from and whither I am going, and when I tell him that I have been travelling in *Hungary* his face brightens up, and pointing to his chest, " *Ich bin von Ungarn*," says he, " *Ich bin von Grosswardein.*"

" Everything comes to him who waits," as the saying goes, and we are at last rewarded for our patience by the opening of the gate which has been erected at the mouth of the grotto. There is something very interesting in visiting such a place as this. Two men with candles in their hands precede you, and anon, extra candles are set fire to that you may see the more clearly a petrified likeness of something such as a dog, a bishop, or a curtain. The river *Poik* rushes with frantic fury through both the old and new grottos; he must be of stupendous depth—a stone thrown into his waters takes such a long time in reaching the bottom. Having picked up some stones as *souvenirs*, I came away and left ADELSBERG for TRIESTE—What a beautiful descent it is from NABRESINA to TRIESTE—*Miramar Castle* stood well out in the clear moonlit sky. At the chief port of the *Adriatic*, I this time tried the Hotel *Delorme*, but can't say that I consider either that or the *Hotel de la ville* to be good enough for so important a place as TRIESTE. I this night saw two drunken men, owing, I suppose, to the presence of the British sailor, " Tom

Bowling," who contaminates every foreign nation he comes across. A traveller cannot but observe this, almost the only drunkenness to be met with on the Continent is in those ports which are frequented by our "Jolly Jack Tar."

Here many women walk about bareheaded with fans in their hands.

The peasant women, as in *Portugal*, carry huge bundles on their heads. On leaving the town an examination of luggage takes place, TRIESTE being a free port. A short journey to GÖRZ, where I go to the *Hotel de la Poste* and drink some good local wine called *Pinot*. Nothing else to remark about this place, which I leave at ten o'clock the following morning.

CHAPTER XV.

NORTHERN ITALY.

WE are soon in *Italy*, and I notice a strong smell of oil at all the railway stations. There is a great difference between this country and the one we have just left. A general appearance of dirtiness here, especially at the stations. The refreshments, however, many of which are handed round by waiters as the trains pull up, are more choice than those in *Austria*. PADUA *(Italian, Padova)* is

ARCADE AT MILAN.

reached at 3.30, and I take the omnibus belonging to the Hotel *Fanti Stella d'oro*, situated on the *Piazza Garibaldi*; just in front of the dining-room window, which after the custom of the country is upstairs, stands a splendid statue of the Great Italian Liberator from whom the square takes its name. PADUA is a very ancient town with many arcades, quite an interesting old place.

In the morning I am awoke early by a tremendous ringing of church bells ; for breakfast they bring me such nasty coffee that I would fain not drink it, but am persuaded to do so, as goodness knows if their tea would be any better. Between PADUA and MILAN we pass for some distance quite near to the shore of lake *Garda* and have magnificent views of that fine sheet of water. At MILAN *(Italian, Milano)* I go to the *Grand hotel de Milan.* This hotel has not a good situation; the street is not rich in shops ; the *Hotel de la ville* has a better position. The electric light is throughout the house, which is so much to be preferred to that horrid heating gas. They register luggage in this hotel. I noticed that the number of my room was on both sides of the door, a capital idea. They give you very good bread in Italy, but their coffee is abominable. I noticed that the police here and also at GENOA wore tall hats like our English constables used to do not so many years ago. They gave me that stuff which goes by the name of " Swiss honey" and which you find in almost all the hotels in *Switzerland*, a kind of treacle, but nevertheless good, The eggs too were very fresh. How grand the arcade here is! I never saw its equal, THE cathedral I will say nothing about as everybody knows it.

After passing some fine mountain and river scenery we arrive at GENOA in a fearful downpour of rain, and the rear portion of the train, in which my carriage is situated, being outside the covered part of the station, I get quite a ducking after stepping out of the compartment. I went to the *Hotel Isotta*, where I was given a handsomely-furnished room, but charged a high price for it. Here began what continued pretty much during the remainder of my wanderings —the mysterious disappearance of the chamber-maid. I only saw her once at GENOA, I saw her once at VENTIMIGLIA, I saw her once at AVIGNON, no such person existed at ARLES, no such person existed at BARCELONA, she appeared again at LERIDA, she did not exist at ZARAGOZA, she was present at CASTEJON, she was also present at BURGOS, she appeared in great force at VALLADOLID, for having occasion to leave my room for a few minutes, upon my return I found it in the possession of three women and a child. This custom of a man fumbling about my room I do not like. I suppose this fellow at GENOA was so busy making beds that he was forced to neglect his shoe cleaning, for that part of his business was very badly done. I found that my shoes were usually the best cleaned at the smallest places I put up at. Hotels are dear in *Italy*. At MILAN no soup could be had under 1 franc 50 centimes From the hotel *Isotta* a door opens on to the arcade which, it being a wet evening, was crowded

with people, but all men—not a woman to be seen, and when
I had an opportunity of seeing the female portion of the
population they were about as plain-looking a lot as I have
met with anywhere. GENOA I thought a very fine town, but
noisy, not unlike TRIESTE in appearance—particularly near
the sea. I took my supper the first night at a restaurant in
the arcade and drank a good bottle of *Barbera* for which I
paid 1 franc 50 centimes, the same kind of wine but of an
inferior quality was charged 3 francs at the hotel. I was
also charged an absurdly high price for candles—what a
swindle this is! and yet it exists everywhere in *Continental
Europe* I believe, except in *Spain* and *Portugal*. I have been
told that even at the *North Cape* at a time of year when midnight is as light as day, candles are charged for in the bills.
They charged me at GENOA two francs for two candles.
Now, supposing that one room should be every night
occupied by a different person, one candle might last a fortnight, in which case it would fetch fourteen francs, and I
suppose the original cost would be at the outside but ten
centimes. That would be doing business at the rate of
14,000 per cent. An idea once occurred to me that I would
not be done over the candles and I set out from *England* with
a good supply in my possession, but this plan only succeeded
when I arrived at an hotel in the day time; on such
occasions I got them to strike the *Bougie* item off my bill.
But you frequently reach your destination after dark, in
which case there is no escape from the imposition, for a
waiter always accompanies you to your room, and the first
thing he does is to light a candle, which once lit you are
bound to pay for. One cannot unpack one's candles in the
dark; you might carry a candle always in your pocket, but
that would not do in warm weather as my experience taught
me, for I had not been touring about long before I found that
my candles were disporting themselves in all sorts of odd
places—some were in my shoes, some had adhered to my
clothes, whilst others had firmly attached themselves like
limpets to the sides of the box.

Another stupid custom, and one that exists more to
our detriment in *England* than anywhere else, is the charge
for attendance, notwithstanding which one is expected to
"tip" the servants as well. In *England*, 1s. 6d. is the usual
charge *per* head. I have a few times, at small places, been
charged only 1s., but, as a rule, a small inn has the same
charge in this respect as a large hotel. A *franc* is the usual
charge in *Switzerland, France, Belgium,* and *Italy*, and about
the same amount in *Germany* and *Hungary*. And a mean
trick—as that is the name it deserves—was resorted to at the

Isotta. Each bill had already printed on it a charge for the receipt stamp. They might as well make one pay for the paper the bill has been made out on. I found the same at BARCELONA at the hotel *Four Nations,* but nowhere else during this tour.

CHAPTER XVI.

CRUELTY TO ANIMALS.

THE morning after my arrival I walked to SESTRI-PONENTE, a kind of suburb of Genoa. The day was beautifully sunny and warm, but my pleasure was spoilt by the incessant cracking of whips, the Italians like the French being excessively fond of noise, only the French merely crack their whips for the sake of the noise, whilst the Italians furiously lash their horses as well, I have never elsewhere seen such cruelty in public places as in *Italy*. I remember once as I was on board steamer, on the lake of *Como*, seeing an overloaded donkey fall to the ground. Its driver began to kick it in its stomach instead of relieving it of its load, and affording it a fair opportunity of regaining its legs. But I hate all forms of cruelty, whether perpetrated by drivers or sportsmen, or vivisectors, or by anybody else! As to what goes by the name of "sport" I take this opportunity of entering a protest against the whole of it. I can see no justification for combining our amusement with the pain or destruction of any creatures, however insignificant such may be. *Napoleon* said of the English that they were a nation of *shopkeepers*; I say they are a nation of *butchers*. The average Englishman seems to be most happy when occupying himself with slaughter; his greatest idea of pleasure is to deprive of its existence some species of the animal creation generally considered to be inferior to himself. The taste is essentially low and degrading, and it is the duty of parents to so educate their children that they may grow up to have a horror of doing anything which may tend to cause suffering to other beings less capable of protecting themselves. Some kinds of sport, such as hunting and coursing, ought to be put down by the strong arm of the law. A bill to prohibit the shooting of birds from traps passed the House of Commons six years ago by a very large majority, but unfortunately the Lords threw it out.

As to vivisectors they perform their evil deeds in dark places, and so do not attract the public attention; but we know from their own writings and confessions what *thoroughgoing fiends* some of them are.

Societies of kindly-disposed persons have been formed for the purpose of arresting the growing tendency towards vivisection. At the present time when the scare of hydrophobia is abroad, an opposition institution has sprung up under the patronage of the Lord Mayor (1889-90) and heir-apparent—this is much to be regretted. I esteem it to be the duty of those who enroll themselves as ministers of the Christian religion to protest against this fearful iniquity in season and out of season, and I consider a clergyman who wilfully neglects to raise his voice against this frightful persecution of the animal world to be nothing less than a traitor to his calling—a minister in fact of the devil and not of the Gospel at all. And yet I have heard of members of the ecclesiastical profession not only paying no attention to this subject, but actually siding with this horrible combination of mercilessness and materialism. A person holding so-called "religious" services in some part of LONDON once advertised in a newspaper that he would preach a sermon *in favour of legitimate vivisection*, and announced that *an anthem would be sung suitable to the occasion.*

It is incomprehensible to my mind how any persons possessing ever so small an amount of humane feeling can bring themselves to regard with unconcern the malpractices of these ruthless tormenters of " man's most faithful friends," (for dogs are in more request for experimental purposes than any other animals). Vivisectors should be shunned by everyone else; they should be made to feel themselves outcasts; they should be taught that their fiendish rites cannot be celebrated without awakening in the hearts of all Christian people a sentiment of horror and disgust. Where possible medical men, opposed to the practice, should be called in at Parliamentary elections, candidates should be sounded as to their views on the subject, for it is a great moral question which deserves much more serious attention than has ever yet been given to it. For my own part, I entertain an instinctive dislike to cruel people, and feel irritated when in their presence. I moreover consider this feeling to be a proper one; and see no reason why we should disemble and make any attempt to conceal those merciful tendencies which have been bestowed upon us by the Great Creator; and when the objects of our sympathy

---

* " An anthem would be sung suitable to the occasion," the occasion being the preaching of a sermon "in favour of legitimate vivisection." What could this mean ? Had this extraordinary person invented some special kind of music which would portray for the *benefit* of his congregation the agonised howls of the animals undergoing torture at the vivisector's hands ?

are dumb animals, unable to plead in their own behalf, there is surely no reason why we should be sparing in the anathemas we may hurl at the heads of those who transgress against the purest feelings of our nature.

NOTE.

Since the above was in type, I have discovered that it was in 1888-9 that the Lord Mayor wished to found a Pasteur Institute, and not in the years quoted on page 50.

CHAPTER XVII.

SOUTH OF FRANCE AND NORTH OF SPAIN.

I LEFT GENOA and arrived at VENTIMIGLIA, the last Italian place on the *Riviera*, but the hotel accommodation, though dear was very poor, and glad I was to get out of it! The town is exceedingly old and beautiful; and a full moon was shining in the clear blue sky as I sauntered over the bridge which crosses the river and divides one part of VENTIMIGLIA from the other. A perpetual snow mountain is visible from this bridge, something like the *Jungfrau* in appearance. (By the way, I hope they will succeed in making a railway up the *Jungfrau*, as then there will be a chance of my getting to the top of it.)

I may mention that mosquito curtains were all around my bed at VENTIMIGLIA, and at one or two places along this route I heard the buzzing of that tiresome little insect. I found the *Mediterranean* to be really of a deep blue colour and not a "gay deceiver" like the so-called "Beautiful Blue Danube." I never before had seen such a clear sky and brilliantly-coloured water; the buildings and hills stood out in grand relief against the sky—it was a lovely sight. All the route as far as MARSEILLES is well worth a visit —each place being more or less beautiful. We passed close under MONTE CARLO with its gamblers and *gourmands* and arrived in good time at MARSEILLES. I put up at the *Hotel du Louvre et de la Paix;* here a chambermaid made her appearance. This was a somewhat expensive hotel; a great many people, mostly English, spend a night here and go on next day by steamer to various places, and when a stranger who leaves his couch at a tolerably comfortable hour goes down to breakfast he finds that the hotel is nearly devoid of visitors. The weather was exceedingly warm along the *Riviera* and at MARSEILLES. I did not like MARSEILLES, there was such a noise—the cracking of whips there is terrific! The streets are dirty, and there are no shops worth looking at. However, I took a walk by the sea which was very pleasant, and visited the grounds of a great *château* where *Napoleon III.* used to stay,

A WOMAN OF ARLES.

but which is now closed. I found two good pianos in the hotel, as I had also done at the *Isotta* at GENOA. Their wine was not good, I found better at the *Maison d'Oree* restaurant close by. A journey of about three-quarters-of-an-hour to ARLES. *Hotel du Nord*. Noticed *Zouaves* about—thought they had been abolished with the Empire. Curious caps on women's heads. Weather windy and cooler. Bad sanitation in hotel. Good piano. Visited Roman amphitheatre and cathedral. A very old town, wretchedly paved. Visited catacombs under hotel, now used as wine cellar, where are to be seen bones (of Christian martyrs I believe.) At the amphitheatre I was informed by the guide that bull-fighting takes place where formerly the Christians and wild beasts fought together in deadly combat. This piece of information together with the guide's incessant chatter about the bulls so disgusted me that I gave him a smaller fee than he evidently expected. A journey of one hour brought me to AVIGNON,* where I found a largish hotel, and the English language spoken. Here we had fires in the evening, the first I had seen since leaving the *North of England*, in September. The hotel *d'Europe* is an old house, three centuries I believe, and it has been an hotel one hundred years. The bedroom doors are so puzzling!—you have to turn the keys and handles the wrong way. It was cold at this place. I had a good luncheon at the *Restaurant des Gourmets* in the principal street, but it was really quite painful to walk about, the pavements were so villainous! The next day some very near relations arrived, and we took a drive over the river *Rhone* which here flows in two parts. The coffee at the hotel was wretched stuff, the tea being much better. Leaving AVIGNON in the afternoon, in less than half-an-hour's time we reach TARASCON, where it is necessary to change trains, unless one is prepared to wait three-and-a-half hours at ARLES which, having just seen that place, I did not feel inclined to do. So, after taking leave of my relations, who were going along the main route, I quitted the train at TARASCON, arrived at CETTE at 10.45, and had three-and-a-half hours to wait there. During this time I visited a *Cafe Chantant* and heard one good singer. Upon arriving, at four o'clock the next morning, at PORTBOU, the frontier station in *Spain*, I found my luggage had not come with me, and so had to leave the keys with a custom-house officer, that he might forward my things after me. It was soon easy to see that we had arrived in *Spain*, by the slow rate at which we moved along. At 10.30 we were at BARCELONA,† and I soon became well-pleased with that lively bright city. There is a very fine statue of *Columbus* near the

---

* See Appendix I.   † See Appendix II.

avenue of palms, and not far from the water and the *Rambla*, a long promenade in the middle of the main street affords a delightful lounge. The people are good-looking, and the shops prettily arranged. We suffered from a plague of flies, the weather being very mild. Leading out of the *Rambla* are some arcades which reminded me of the *Palais Royal* at PARIS. On the Saturday I left BARCELONA a flower market was being held on the *Rambla*, and I noticed some very large strawberries in a shop window. This day we passed within view of the monastery of *Montserrat*, but I did not stop until I got to LERIDA,* where my previous visits to *Spain* were immediately recalled to mind by the numerous balconies in front of the windows of all the houses. The carriages on this line are constructed so as to carry ten persons each. Living is cheap at the Spanish country *fondas*. They always put you *en pension* however short your stay may be; but I am told that should you only occupy your room and have no refreshment in the house the charge is just the same. *Table d'hôte* meals are the order of the day, and wine is always included—it is not always good, however, and generally very heavy. On the way to ZARAGOZA blind guitar players took up positions at some of the stations. In *Spain* one is always struck by the tremendous noise at the stations; people shout at the tops of their voices, and everybody seems to be talking at the same time. At ZARAGOZA the shouting of the omnibus men was most extraordinary—I never heard such a peculiar wailing. *En route* we saw in the distance the snow-capped *Pyrenees* and shivered as we contemplated this wintry scene. Omnibus travelling in Spain is expensive, the conveyances not belonging to the hotels. I was generally charged 1 peseta 50 cents each way, whereas in Austria the fare was usually but sixpence. Every train is accompanied by two *gens d'armes* armed with rifles. At many towns the watchman's voice may be heard, his shrill cry echoing through the stillness of the night. Good butter is not to be obtained in *Spain* or *Portugal* either without paying an enormous price for it; but the worst part of travelling in these countries is the appalling dirtiness of the people; in their domestic habits they are filthy, and the sanitary arrangements atrocious;—enough to debar any person at all fastidiously inclined from paying a second visit. However, in ANDALUCIA this is not so much the case. Beggars are numerous almost everywhere—it is shameful that the Spaniards and Portuguese allow such people to go abont—but the governments of these countries actually sell them licenses to beg. At ZARAGOZA† I discovered two things, each of which I considered to be about the finest

---

* See Appendix III. † See Appendix IV.

specimen of its kind I had ever seen, viz.—the cathedral (the newest of the two), and the *Grand café de Ambos Mundos*. This latter has the reputation of being the largest in *Spain*, I have never seen so large an one in any country. The cathedral *Nuéstra Senóra del Pilar* is a magnificent building said to be the third largest in *Spain*. I have not been to TOLEDO, but this of ZARAGOZA made a far greater impression upon me than the famous one at SEVILLE. ZARAGOZA also possesses a leaning tower. The town resembles GRANADA in appearance. The morning after my arrival a parade of troops passed my window. There were lancers and artillery, the gun-carriages of the latter being drawn by mules.

ZARAGOZA CATHEDRAL.

At the hotel I found a very commodious sponge bath, quite an unusual thing to meet with anywhere on the Continent. Continuing my journey I came to a station called CASTEJON, where there seemed to be but a few cottages about. This place is a junction for PAMPLONA and ALSASUA, the shortest way to reach the main line between IRUN and MADRID if one is going north; but as I was going south, my nearest way was straight on to MIRANDA. I found very comfortable quarters at CASTEJON and enjoyed a nice little supper consisting of fish, eggs, ham, cheese, fruit, coffee, and excellent beer from SAN SEBASTIAN. I was shown to a house across the railway, and spent the night in a very clean bedroom with a handsome clock upon the mantelpiece, which as usual, however, was at a standstill (throughout this tour scarcely a clock but had stopped, and on one occasion I was told that this article of furniture, which can be of so much use, was merely there for ornament) and eight chairs, two of them being armchairs. Was I expected to hold a *levée*: if so, where were the people to come from? In the morning I was up early and breakfasted off coffee and cold sausages, and my bill altogether only amounted to five *pesetas* (four shillings.) I believe it to be the best plan if you want to break your journey in *Spain*, always to go to the *Fondas* at the railway stations, they are very clean, and you get better food at the refreshment *buffets* than you are likely to do in the village inns or hotels of provincial towns, but you only find these convenient places at junctions. The traveller is much amused upon arriving at a restaurant to find arranged on the table small coffee cups filled half-way up with lumps of sugar. The Spaniards are so fond of sweet things, they even eat sugar with ham. You may travel for many a mile in a mountainous country and never meet with a tunnel. I had during these last few days very pleasant Spaniards as travelling companions.

CHAPTER XVIII.

SOME OLD SPANISH TOWNS.

AT Burgos I put up at the *Hotel del Norte*, and for the first time came across a waitress in the dining-room! The people here spoke French, and I joined a *table d'hôte* dinner and ordered a bottle of *Val de Peñas*, but this I found to be far too alcoholic for my diminished head. The following morning, as in duty bound, I paid a visit to the cathedral, and joined a party being shown round, and was getting to be very tired of hearing so much talk of people of whom I knew and cared nothing when all at once the priests struck up a tremendous Gregorian roaring, a noise that always exasperates me. Was Pope *Gregory* really the inventer of these most unmusical sounds? I saw the coffin of the *Cid*, soon after which the guide informed me that he had finished and wanted to pass me on to another man, but I retorted that I also had finished and slipped a *peseta* into his hand for which he did not even thank me. These old Spanish towns have usually arcades which must be very convenient in rainy weather. A four hour's ride by rail brought me to VALLADOLID, where I went to the hotel *Giglo*, and found both French and English spoken there. They gave me a very spacious bedroom, from which I was surprised to hear the sound of a barrel organ in the street. Such things being very rare out of *Great Britain*. They don't, as a rule, tolerate these disturbers of the public quiet in foreign towns. There was nothing much to be seen at VALLADOLID and I had to leave at the awkward hour of 11.39 p.m., arriving at SALAMANCA at four o'clock in the morning. It was cold travelling through the night, the country about here being two thousand feet or more above the level of the sea. At the *Fonda del Comeras* I got a big bedroom with large washing basin, and lay down for a few hours' sleep. At eight o'clock a waiter brought me up some red-coloured Spanish chocolate—a thing I detest is chocolate! So to the surprise of the man I told him to take it away, and hearing a great noise outside my window peeped out when, behold! there was an omnibus with three horses abreast, and they were trying to harness a donkey in front of them! My thermometer was as low as

44 degrees *Fahrenheit* at nine a.m., the coldest temperature I had experienced since leaving SALZBURG. I walked through the old town: it is a most interesting place; the cathedral is a grand one; and the carving over the front entrance is very delicate. The whole appearance of SALAMANCA* is interesting. I went on to a common and came across a large flock of gingerbread coloured sheep, a white one being dispersed here and there. In the evening I took train to CIUDAD RODRIGO, a very old town, where I arrived late, and went to the hotel *Mirobrigense*. What an entrance this place had! I could see in the dark that there were pools of muddy water about the

SALAMANCA CATHEDRAL.

court-yard. An old-fashioned stone staircase led up into such bewildering passages! sounds of music and revelry greeted my ears, and I came to a room containing a multitude of people listening to a performance on the *pianoforte*. I am conducted past this through a room where there is a gallery and theatrical stage, I take a turn to the right, a turn to the left, and so on, until at last I arrive at the apartment that has been allotted to my use, a fine room, very, with two alcoves, each containing a bed and washandstand; there are sofa, armchairs, table, and other furniture in the room. My

---

* See Appendix V.

luggage is carried by four men, I myself being accompanied by the landlord, an old man in a skull cap smoking a cigarette, and a waiter. A fat woman is busy putting one of the beds to rights. Two of the men who have carried the luggage remain transfixed as it were or fascinated by something—they show no sign of any intention to leave the room. As I cannot make anything of any of these people nor they of me, another couple of men appear on the scene, one of whom makes a polite bow and addresses me in French; after thanking my interpreter he leaves the room, but not so the man who had come with him, and whom I believe to have been the landlord's son, not so the old landlord himself who still puffs away at his cigarette, not so the fat woman who still is occupied with the bed, nor the waiter, who is evidently waiting for orders, nor the two men who have helped to carry the luggage, these latter from what I am able to make out want to know if my boxes contain merchandise for disposal. I unlock one box and begin to take out the things necessary for the night, and don't all these people stare at me and into the box! I go to one of the washandstands and prepare to make myself comfortable after my journey (the fat woman in the meantime having disappeared), but there they stand, no one seems to think of leaving the room, and a considerable amount of time elapses before I am left alone to "arrange my toilet," to use what I always consider a rather stiff sort of phraseology. By this time I am pretty hungry; it is eleven o'clock, and my last meal was at mid-day, so I thread my way through the labyrinth of passages and eventually arrive at the *Comedor*. The first thing brought to me is an omelette, but when I taste it I find it has been cooked in oil, so I let the waiter take it away; then follows some liver, same thing, oil again; then beef, same again, all oil; then partridge, same again. The waiter appears to be concerned that I do not eat, but I manage with cheese, biscuits, and fruit to appease my appetite and retire to my spacious quarter where I actually find a piece of soap, and there were salt spoons on the dinner table! Extraordinary combinations of civilization and primitiveness are to be found in some of the out-of-the-way parts of *Europe*. I find this place is used as a *Casino*, and on the night of my arrival they were having a concert and ball. When I see the courtyard by daylight it looks even dirtier than I could have believed. A coat-of-arms is over the portal—the house had probably been the residence of some important personage in former days. Wishing to get out of this place as soon as possible, as I can get scarcely anything that I am able to eat, and as, after making a survey of the town, I find there is nothing whatever to see, and as there is only one train a day in the direction I want to go, which train leaves at 7.20 in the morning, which would necessitate my being disturbed from my slumbers at five as I have felt too tired to hurry off the morning after my arrival and do not wish to spend another night in this extraordinary establishment, I express a wish that I may be driven to VILLA FORMOSO, the frontier town of *Portugal*, twenty-five kilometres distant. From what I can make out I am given to understand that my "turn out" will be ready at the appointed time, and so determine to breakfast off cold sausage and boiled eggs, through the shells of which the oil cannot penetrate. I also enjoy some more sausage and German beer later on in the forenoon, and begin to grow impatient that my carriage does not arrive, when upon looking through the window, which opens upon the courtyard, I destry two donkeys. It appears that this is the way in which I am to travel. My luggage is fastened on to the back of one ass, and the driver fastens the two asses together with a rope which he leads and I walk at the side, and in this way I take my departure from *Roderick's* historical city. Most certainly did this place we had just left fulfill the saying, that "distance lends enchantment to the view," for on looking back on CIUDAD RODRIGO I was lost in admiration of its beauties. We had crossed a river and reached a plain, a dreary uninhabited sort of country, when the driver asked me to mount the spare donkey, but preferring to walk I declined the invitation, and we had not proceeded much further on our way when the driver himself jumped upon its back and thus we continued for I should say six miles or more until we came to a stream that it was necessary to ford. With difficulty the driver helped me on to the donkey (he himself afterwards mounting the one carrying the luggage) for there were no stirrups, nor were there reins, only a rope tied on the left side of the donkey's head wherewith to guide that "fiery steed," for such he soon proved himself to be, as upon approaching a cavalcade of his fellow-creatures, he increased his speed till he got into a canter, and finally into a galop, and I had much difficulty in pulling him up, but after tugging away at the rope I succeeded in bringing his head round, whereupon I could almost imagine that he gave me a look after the manner of the *Blondin donkey*, which my readers may have seen performing on the tight rope at the Crystal Palace, *Sydenham*, or Royal Aquarium, *Westminster*. After this I dismounted, and we continued our journey as we had begun it. We passed great numbers of olive trees, but met scarcely any people. Darkness set in, and we were at a loss as to which way to take until a man offered to guide us, and eventually we arrived at the railway station of FUENTES DE OÑORO, the last one in *Spain*. I wanted to go to the first in *Portugal*, but was told that it was too late to cross the frontier that night. At the *Fonda* they brought to me, as interpreter, a very pretty little girl of about twelve years of age. She spoke French fluently, and I was escorted to my night's lodging—a small house across the railway. I was on this occasion accompanied by a lot of people, there being besides my interpreter two smaller girls, her sisters, a boy, two men, and a woman; here occurred a scene somewhat similar to what had taken place at CIUDAD RODRIGO. There were two small rooms, the bed being in the one furthest from the door, the woman busied herself arranging the bed, and all the rest remained with me in the other room standing staring at my proceedings, as I opened my box to unpack the things necessary for the night. If I desired anything I had only to express my wants in French and little *Mercedes*, for that was her name, saw that it was immediately forthcoming. The following morning I left FUENTES DE ONORO and travelled in a very dirty carriage as far as PAMPILHOSA, the junction for OPORTO. The route was picturesque. Gigantic boulders were lying about, and the country was well-wooded, so different from *Spain*, where one scarcely ever sees a tree (other than fruit trees), and *France*, where the trees are usually mere stumps. *Portugal* more resembles *Italy* than any other country with which I am acquainted. When we approached the splendid bridge over the *Douro*, which is one of *M. Eiffel's* achievements, a thick mist had enveloped the city so that I was disappointed, and could not see that wonderful view. The line being a single one we seem to be suspended in mid-air—the height above the river must be something like two hundred feet.

I will now take leave of my readers for a space as I feel confident that ere this they have provided themselves with my " Winter and Spring in Spain and Portugal " wherein they will find a somewhat minute description of the great port wine city.

CHAPTER XIX.

SOUTH OF PORTUGAL.

A JOURNEY of one-and-a-half hours from OPORTO by what in this country goes by the name of an express, that is to say a train that travels at the rate of something under thirty miles an hour, brings us to AVEIRO. This is a large village situated on a canal, which communicates with the sea. The neighbourhood abounds in beautiful women, an unusual occurrence in *Portugal*, where there is usually a very great contrast to the handsome faces so frequently met with in *Spain*. Long boats after the manner of Venetian gondolas and manned by men, who in their costumes much resemble their Venetian brethren, go backwards and forwards on the canal, and we may, without a greater degree of exaggeration than is customary in such cases, describe AVEIRO as being the " Venice of Portugal." Frugal accommodation is to be had at the *Hotel Central*, but the place is hardly worthy of a visit.

We found LISBON (*Portuguese*, LISBOA) in a disturbed state. The influenza epidemic was raging, and the streets were thronged with funeral processions,* the priests riding in Sedan chairs drawn by mules. Also the embalmed body of the *Empress* of *Brazil* arrived a few days after we got to LISBON, and was deposited in the church of *S. Vicente de Fora*, where all the members of the Portuguese royal family find a last resting place. We drove to the church, but the crowd was so great going to see the corpse of the late king, that we were unable to obtain admittance. How badly off this city is in the way of hotel accommodation ! We stayed at the *Universal*, which has a central position, facing the *Rua do Chiado*, the principal street, at the top of which a fine statue of *Camoens* has recently been put up. This house was conducted on the *pension* system. Breakfast from nine to one, before the former hour the *Salle-à-manger* being closed, and the same again from two to six, when dinner is served, which meal being over, the room is again locked up. This was

---

* In OPORTO funerals take place at night, a capital plan, which might be adopted with advantage everywhere else.

VIEW OF LISBON.

GENERAL VIEW OF CINTRA.

absurd! The Portuguese have the most wonderful appetites of any people I ever came across. It is their custom to eat a *dejeuner à la fourchette* at nine o'clock. They will at that early hour indulge in such heavy food as beef-steaks and potatoes, pork chops, &c., washed down by their native wines and followed by coffee, and anyone wishing for an English breakfast has difficulty in getting what he wants, as they don't understand our drinking coffee together with solid food, and you either have to go through your meal parched with thirst or else let it get cold before the coffee arrives. We dined the first night at the *table d' hôte*, but the atmosphere was so stifling and the waiters had been forbidden to open any of the windows, that we were obliged to quit the table before our meal was over, and finish it in a private room. There was only one clock in this hotel, and that was at a standstill after the manner of the inhabitants, who are a sleepy lot. The natives are notorious for their plain looks. The climate is warmer than at OPORTO, and the houses are built without fire-places or stoves, or any other means of producing artificial warmth. The town is very hilly and dirty, and bad smells are wafted on the breeze, but in this respect LISBON is no match for OPORTO which, with the solitary exception of VENICE, is the foulest smelling city I ever was at. One morning we took train to CINTRA, a place of much beauty, and afterwards hired a conveyance and drove *via* MONTSERRAT and COLLARES (noted for its wine) to *Cape Roca*, the Westernmost point in *Europe*. The rocks about here reminded me of the scenery in JERSEY. A steamer plies across the Tagus and a train meets it and conveys the passengers either on to FARO or to SETUBAL, which latter is an hour-and-a-quarter distant. Hither accompanied by a brother-in-law (not the invalid before mentioned) I set off, and acting on the advice of the driver of the carriage we had hired at the railway station, we went to the *Hotel de Paris*, which had the tricolour flying from one of its topmost windows. The entrance was up a narrow lane down which flowed a veritable flood of filth, and inside the doorway and up the dark, gloomy staircase, we could detect foul odours. SETUBAL has a fine fish-market in which *plaice* can be bought at one penny per pound, and large sardines cost twopence half-penny a dozen. We visited two or three places where they were packing the sardines: the process is interesting. We saw the sardines steeped in boiling oil and afterwards put into the tins which we also saw being constructed. A great many French people live in SETUBAL, being employed in the sardine trade. The position of SETUBAL is beautiful. A good military band was practising some cheerful music, and the sun shone with vigour. After lunching at the *hotel Français*, a much cleaner house than that at which we were staying, and partaking of a cup of good coffee at the smaller *hotel Setubalense* we left for FARO. At 10.30 p.m. we arrived at BEJA and enjoyed a nicely-cooked supper at the railway refreshment room. *Bass's Pale Ale* being in prime condition. A cold journey brought us in the early morn to the picturesque valley of *Monchique* (this name has quite a French sound, and so has *Loule*, which we pass later on, not long before reaching FARO.) No foot warmers are supplied to passengers on this line, and we got to our destination in a shivering condition. At the inn we had much difficulty in rousing anybody up, but after being kept waiting a considerable time, were shown into a couple of rooms communicating with each other. This proved to be a dirty place. Beggars in a loathsome condition crawled about the staircase. The sea was some way out, leaving at low-tide a sort of morass, and I should say that FARO would be a first-rate place for anybody to go to who should wish to become inflicted with ague or malaria. I soon sickened of it and ordered a carriage to take me on to VILLA REAL, the last town in *Portugal*. This turned up at the time appointed, but it was a closed carriage; and wishing to sit outside so as to enjoy the open air, the driver at my instigation tried to put my box inside, but the doorway was too narrow, then I suggested that it should be tied by a rope behind on a place that seemed to be there for the purpose, but my brother-in-law, more farseeing than myself, objected that some one might *cut the rope*, and I had after all to take my seat in the interior. At OLHÃO, a few miles distant, I took leave of my companion, and continued my journey alone. How low-lying the country about here is! At one part the sea appeared to be on the top of a hill. We passed many carts with canvas covers, which were painted in various colours, and jogged along leisurely until we came to TAVIRA, where I had some refreshment and a change of horses took place, a mule being substituted for one of them, and this seemed to answer well, for the driver having refreshed himself at a tavern became quite elated, sang in the idiotic manner common amongst the Portuguese, and finally touched up his quadrupeds, who got into a galop, and we went along at a merry speed. Chancing to look back, I discerned a magnificent sunset, and told the driver to pull up that I might enjoy this beatific vision. Towards seven o'clock we arrived at VILLA REAL, and I put up at the *hotel Hispanhol*, kept by a Spaniard, which I found to be a clean little place. Most of the houses in this town had but one story; they were white-washed and presented a smart appearance. I was agreeably surprised to find placed before me at supper a bottle of *Tennant's stout*, which was in capital condition. In the morning I surveyed VILLA REAL, but there was not much to be seen. In the square was a monument to *José I.*, who reigned in the last century. This told of his being "the restorer of "the arts and sciences, the protector of the oppressed, " the promoter of commerce, the friend of peace," and in fact everything that would lead one to believe him to have been a most exemplary sovereign! On looking out of the dining-room window I saw a little girl cleaning boots on a house-top.

CHAPTER XX.

SOUTH-WEST ANDALUCIA.

THE view of AYAMONTE across the mouth of the *Guadiana* is very picturesque. Half-an-hour or so's sail brought me to that place, where I took the diligence to GIBRALEON—this journey occupied six hours. On leaving the outskirts of AYAMONTE, a gendarme got into the carriage and travelled with us as far as LEPE; at this place I noticed many beautiful faces; the people were sitting outside their houses basking in the brilliant sunshine. At CARTAJA we stopped a quarter-of-an-hour, and I refreshed myself in a cozy little cottage with eggs, pork, and white wine; three good-looking girls in the meantime sitting down on the steps of the doorway and casting coy glances towards me as I was enjoying my food. I don't think it far from the truth to say that as far as girls and young women were concerned, I never saw an ugly face, and seldom a plain one in this part of *Spain*. At GIBRALEON we took train to HUELVA, distant less than an hour and arrived at the latter place at ten o'clock. How can I describe the comfort I found at the *Colon (Columbus) Hotel!* It is certainly one of the best I have ever met with. The public rooms are so numerous and spacious—there are five *en suite*—billiard, card, smoking, reading, and conversation; (the only other hotel I know that has such a number of public rooms is the *Constanzerhof*, at CONSTANCE), a very lofty dining-room and another, which in the winter is used as a music room, and this measures about *fifty yards* in length. The food consumed in the hotel comes from the farms, which belong to the same company, for this hotel was erected some ten years ago by the *Rio Tinto* Copper-Mining Company. In winter few come here but Englishmen, on their way to and from the mines. The place is devoid of tourists, although the climate could not be more delightful anywhere. A scorching sun shines throughout the day; my thermometer on January 14th registered 60 degrees *Fahrenheit* in my room at five o'clock p.m., and the window was wide open and I had no fire. It would indeed be impossible to over-estimate either the salubrity of the climate or the comfort of the hotel, and I would recommend those English people who every year betake themselves away from their native land, in order to escape the horrors of the winter, to give HUELVA a trial, instead of so assiduously patronizing the *Riviera*, where they are liable to earthquake, wintry weather and the hostile *Mistral*. It is true there is no amusement of any sort to be obtained. There is a small English church and an English doctor.

The only excursion of interest is to the *Rabida Convent*, called *Columbus' House*. That great navigator set sail from close by there on his ever-memorable voyage of discovery. This excursion takes about one-and-a-half hours by sailing boat. The house is the ordinary white-washed, red-tiled building of the district. It is of course very antique. Approaching it from the sea a solitary palm-tree acts as a sentry in front of it. It possesses two court-yards, in which oranges, roses and various plants thrive, and a picture gallery containing mostly portraits of *Columbus* himself. In summertime it is used as an hotel, where people go for the sea-bathing.

There is also a chapel attached to it. the pulpit, gallery, and one of the altars being more than four hundred years old. The caretaker gathered me a couple of red roses, my favourite flower, but I unfortunately dropped them on the way back. HUELVA is only about four hours from SEVILLE, so that it cannot be considered at all an out-of-the way place.

CHAPTER XXI.

SOME INTERESTING PLACES IN ANDALUCIA.

I FOUND the climate of SEVILLE more gloomy than that of HUELVA and set off for CADIZ the day after my arrival at the former place. Having put up at the *Hotel de Paris*, I was comfortably entertained, but upon making a survey of the town my nose was disagreeably affected by the stenches which pervade it. The town is very puzzling to find one's

CADIZ.

way about in. The following morning I walked all round it, and visited the cathedral and tobacco manufactory where fifteen hundred girls and women are employed. At the hotel the walnuts were the finest I ever saw, and it is the custom in this country for the waiter to crack them before placing them upon the table. There was an interesting open-air market, and turkeys were very plentiful in CADIZ. All the houses have flat roofs, and good views can be obtained from them. The weather was dull; the town is too nearly surrounded by water to possess a very dry climate. Within two hours by rail of CADIZ lies JEREZ. Here I tasted a glass of *sherry* as we English call it, and a deliciously-flavoured beverage it was, not at all fiery as we know it in *England*. After traversing the dreary Andalucian plains, a seemingly almost uninhabited part of the world, with occasional views of purple mountains in the distance, we got back to SEVILLE. I found the cathedral undergoing repair. Most people will have heard of the "Barber of Seville;" whether owing to *Figaro* or not, SEVILLE abounds in "barber's" shops. At the *Hotel de Madrid*, the visitor is well-pleased to have an opportunity of tasting fresh butter; this was by far the best I had ever met with in *Spain*, and is brought, I am told, from MADRID. The food at the hotel is very abundant: For luncheon you are given a bill of fare consisting of fifteen hot dishes of which you are allowed to choose three, and the white wine is very nice. What a much better plan of managing hotels the Spaniards have than other nations! You are charged so much a day, wine included. This saves a great deal of trouble as regards booking. Mistakes are prevented and you know what you are spending. Of course baths, fires (if you want such things which is rarely the case), and odd cups of tea or coffee are charged extra. At HUELVA you pay seven shillings a day, and the wine is the best I have ever drank of the ordinary kind. You are there situated in private grounds. You have scarcely any steps to climb, the hotel having but two stories. You find baths and sanitary arrangements as in *England*, the bedrooms are lofty and spacious, possessing the largest description of washing basins, the attendance is prompt, you have the *Times, Graphic, Punch*, and *Pall Mall Budget* to read, you have a lovely grand piano to play upon, and you have shady seats in the quadrangle where you can read or muse as fancy wills, and enjoy in a subdued degree the brilliant sunshine.

Bent upon visiting MALAGA, I left SEVILLE one morning at ten o'clock; a long dreary journey brought me to LA RODA, where I refreshed myself with some wine and a pomegranate.

At BOBADILLA I indulged in some ham and coffee, but the ham had, after the custom of the country, been besprinkled with sugar, and I had some difficulty in eating it. Soon after leaving BOBADILLA we got amongst a wild and rugged type of scenery, huge precipitous rocks rose thousands of feet above us, and I do not remember, even in *Switzerland*, to have seen anything more grand. When we got down to the valley, for many a mile orange, lemon, and occasionally almond trees in blossom skirted the railway track. and when we arrived at MALAGA we had come to a summer climate. They know no winter there, they know no autumn or even spring according to the English ideas of those seasons. They enjoy perpetual summer at MALAGA. To give an idea of the warmth of the climate I have merely to mention that my thermometer outside my window at midnight stood at 58 degrees *Fahrenheit*. This was on the 21st of January. I found the *Hotel de Rome* comfortable but the *salle-à-manger* overpoweringly stuffy. I had a most spacious bedroom allotted to me and altogether had not much to complain of. There was also a lift in the hotel, the only one I had ever seen in *Spain*. This hotel, which formerly bore the name of *Alameda*, is situated at the corner of a street that leads into the *Alameda*. This *Alameda* corresponds to the *Rambla* at BARCELONA, only, it is though broader, not so long, and no well-dressed people are to be seen promenading about. In fact, MALAGA would appear to be a poor town, with many beggars in it, and these flock in large numbers to the door of the hotel whenever any omnibus arrives. The tea and coffee at the hotel were very good. The port of MALAGA somewhat resembles RAMSGATE. A short walk off is a British cemetery, at the gateway of which sit two lions on stone pedestals, emblematical, I suppose, of the "British Lion." There is a bed of a dried up river which is used for a market, but I am told that occasionally the river has its full compliment of water, when the gipsies and others who frequent it for the purpose of hawking their goods are obliged to beat a retreat. They are making a coast line which will connect MALAGA with ALMERIA on the east and GIBRALTAR on the west, and which will eventually extend as far as CADIZ and HUELVA. MALAGA may no doubt be a capital place for people who have spent the better part of their lives in *India* or some other hot climate, but I found it far too relaxing and was glad to leave. The evening before leaving I paid a visit to a *Café Chantant*. The first portion of the programme consisted of a comedy, and this, although I could not understand what was being said, proved to be very amusing. A waiter showed me to a front seat in a gallery facing the stage, and I had not been there long before two girls made their way up to where I was and took their seats beside me. I guessed what they were. One, of about seventeen years of age, very dark, and possessing very bright eyes, asked for wine, and after I had treated herself and her companion to it, the cheeky minx demanded cigarettes, but neither being a smoker myself nor desirous of encouraging the habit in others, especially in members of the female sex, I declined to accede to her request, and the two soon betook themselves off to serenade some other person. After the play was over I was not surprised to see these two girls make their way up on to the stage, and the cheeky bright-eyed one eventually danced with much skill. *They were gipsies.* It was odd to see the natives of MALAGA walk about in their warm, picturesque cloaks, fancying it was winter! At BOBADILLA, which we repass on our way to CORDOVA, one observes foot-warmers ready to be put into those carriages which are destined to go to GRANADA. That place I longed to see again. Nothing could exceed the beauty of the *Alhambra*, and its situation is so magnificent! But there is something that I have reason to believe that many tourists fail to visit and that is the *Cartuja Convent*. The marble there is exquisite and the whole building, although it has not acquired the same reputation as the *Alhambra*, is as well worth seeing in my opinion. But GRANADA is a cold place in winter, and we found when we were there one December, the popular hotel, the *Washington Irving* to be a comfortless place. After leaving BOBADILLA we soon got to a dreary country, nothing in the way of cultivation save olive trees, and there were regular forests of these, extending as far as the eye could reach on both sides of the line. At half-past eight we arrived at CORDOVA.

CHAPTER XXII.

CORDOVA, SEVILLE, AND MERIDA.

IT was not the first time I had visited this quaint old place. The *hotel de Suisse* is kept by a Swiss, and the rooms are large and airey, although the house is somewhat shut in by narrow streets. At supper I was surprised to find placed before me some *Bacalhao*, a dried codfish which the Portuguese are so fond of, and of which the whole of OPORTO smells terribly. There was a stove lighted in the dining-room.

GENERAL VIEW OF CORDOVA.

I learnt that since the attack upon *Dr. Middleton* by the gipsy-guide, those loafers who used to hang about the hotel and so pester travellers are no longer allowed to do so, but notwithstanding this I was very much incommoded the following morning by one of these gentry. I left the hotel for the purpose of going to the cathedral but missed the right turning, and a man with an evil countenance offered to direct me, but, not liking his look, I told him I did not require his assistance. However, he followed me, when I hurried, he hurried, when I stopped, he stopped, when I turned, he turned. At last, getting back to the place where I had first encountered him, I veered off down a promenade called *Gran Capitan*, and walked the length of it, and looking back could see him nowhere about, so I turned back once more, when out he pounced from a house right across my path and followed me as far as the hotel, and kept hovering about outside the entrance, so I got one of the interpreters belonging to the hotel to accompany me a short distance and put me in the right road to the cathedral, and in this manner succeeded in getting rid of my troublesome pursuer. Strangers should have no dealings with these men. At the hotel there are guides who speak the English language, and there is no occasion to employ the casual people one finds on the streets. The way from the hotel to the cathedral is across the road to the right and the first turning on the left, called *Jesus Maria*. (It is the most usual custom in *Spain* merely to put the name of the street and not use the word " Calle," which signifies "street," at all. This is quite different to what obtains in *Italy*, where even each railway station is labelled " Stazioni di, etc.") Follow the gutter which runs down the middle of the street and you cannot go wrong. Coming back I was met by a carriage and pair of horses and was obliged to retreat a few yards to where the street was wider in order that it might pass. I paced the street at the point where I had met the carriage, and it was only about eight feet across. Vehicles are only allowed to go in one direction in these narrow streets, a notice being put up to signify when it is permitted to carriages so drive down a particular street.

There had been heavy rains in CORDOVA and the streets were disagreeably dirty. The only things of interest are, the cathedral, the Roman bridge over the *Guadalquiver*, and two old water-mills in the stream—these all lie near together. The cathedral is quite different to what you would find anywhere else. It possesses I don't know how many red and white pillars : *Bradshaw* says eight hundred, from seven to twelve yards apart. It was first of all a Roman Temple and afterwards a Moorish Mosque. The tower stands apart from the main building, a courtyard with two palm and many orange trees intervening. I was amused to see a little cripple with a stick to lean upon : he flung his stick at an orange tree, knocked off an orange, picked it up, and hobbled away with a smile of satisfaction upon his countenance. The Swiss hotel at CORDOVA has its name over the entrance in five different languages, viz.: *English, French, German, Italian*, and *Spanish*, and it would be well for every school-boy to learn these five languages, and let *Greek* and *Latin* go to the wall. Education as carried out in *England* is most unpractical and very often one who has been to a public school or private tutor has, upon attaining to manhood, to begin his education all over again. This is not as it should be, and parents are very much to blame for allowing themselves to be duped into educating their sons according to the dictates of some fusty old fogies who have a pecuniary interest in keeping up this rotten state of things. However, as matters are at present, Lawyers and doctors require *Latin* and clergy certainly ought

INTERIOR OF CORDOVA CATHEDRAL.

to know *Greek* and *Hebrew* too, in my opinion, so as to be able to read the scriptures in the languages in which they were originally written. This was the only hotel, since I had entered *Spain*, where I did not find the usual mosquito curtains, for at every place I stopped at I was more or less worried by the buzzing of that troublesome insect. The route from CORDOVA to SEVILLE is more interesting than that from SEVILLE to BOBADILLA. ALMODOVAR is a village that clusters round and clambers up a hill, on the top of which are the remains of a Moorish castle. This, I thought, the most picturesque old ruin I had ever seen of the kind, and a fellow-passenger agreed with me. Upon my return to SEVILLE, I got a bedroom at the *sucursal* or *dependence* of the hotel—this proved more sunny and spacious than the one I had before occupied. This *dependence* is a very comfortable place. There is a reading-room with piano in it, and one is left more to oneself than in the corresponding room at the hotel. I would, however, recommend anyone purporting to visit this place to avoid No. III. and the adjoining rooms, as just across the street is a church bell which is a very great nuisance. In the evening I went to a *café* in the *Sierpes*. The performance begun at seven o'clock and did not finish till past midnight. The first portion of the entertainment was uninteresting. There were some eighteen or twenty gipsy girls and women with four men playing guitars, and a very tall, stout, clean-shaven elderly man, who appeared to possess ever so many double chins. He is armed with a stick after the pattern of a conductor's *bâton* and this he keeps almost perpetually beating, either against his own leg or against that of the chair on which he is sitting, whilst, now and again, he will give a twitch with his head after the manner of one suffering from *St Vitus' Dance*. This I suppose he does for the purpose of emphasising the time. Sometimes he will burst out into a most crazy kind of shouting, which, no doubt, he himself would call singing, for these Spaniards have no more real idea of singing than I have of flying. One or two of these people dance at a time and all the rest clap their hands. Towards the conclusion of the dance everybody becomes frantic with excitement, and the screaming and yelling that takes place is most discordant. The latter part of the programme however, which did not begin until after eleven o'clock, was really entertaining. Two girls and a very fat woman, in shockingly short dresses, and a man in Spanish costume danced, whilst a blind man played sweet and graceful airs upon a piano. The dancers had castinets and the effect was quite captivating. After this was finished a play took place, this had a touch of the tragic about it, for there was a figure to represent a child which a man kept banging about and at one time threw right over his head. Afterwards a host of girls, dressed up as men and carrying some peculiar sort of guns, appeared on the scene and struck up a chorus, the music of which was decidedly pretty, but as they all sang through their noses the effect was spoiled.

  The following morning I paid a visit to the Government Tobacco Manufactory: this is the largest in *Spain*. Five thousand girls and women are employed. In one room alone there are said to be 2,500 at work. Amongst them are many gipsies, and taking them all in all they are a very good-looking lot. We saw a very fair-haired little child which had been put into a kind of basket, so constructed that it was able to waddle about, keeping its little self balanced and not upsetting. All those women who are fortunate enough to be mothers have their babies by them in their cradles. As you pass through the numerous rooms where these people are working you frequently encounter fiery glances from dark-eyed beauties, and many appeals are made to you to bestow money upon these merry and cheerful toilers in life. This would be a capital place for a young man on the look out for a wife to come to, and I affirm, without the slightest fear of contradiction, that should he be of a susceptible nature, he would straightway embrace *Mormonism* and quit the establishment, having half-a-dozen dark-eyed damsels dangling on to each arm.*

Amongst all this Southern loveliness occasionally might be seen a *red-haired* maiden. Such a contrast to her surroundings.

In the afternoon I took a walk down the *Delicias*, the fashionable drive and promenade of SEVILLE. There were a few carriages, but mostly closed, although this day the sun shone brilliantly, the sky was clear, and there was perfect stillness in the air. The Spanish ladies are evidently very much afraid of fresh air, and seldom leave their houses except on gala days. At the hotel I never could get enough salt; it is kept in pepper pots, and you have to shake it out: this is a good plan with soup, but it is difficult to get a sufficient quantity on to one's plate to give one's meat a proper relish. The wine is conveyed in pig-skins which give it a nasty flavour.

In the evening my attention was attracted to a small room in the *Calle de Sierpes*, the street which is most full of people, and where the best shops are situated. Having paid one *real*,† I entered and found a camel with two monkeys on its back, and a serpent carefully wrapped up in flannel. This latter, on being disturbed, shot out its fiery tongue; but it appeared to be tame, and allowed itself to be caressed.

Afterwards, I strolled into a café where I had the pleasure of listening to some good music. A fair-looking young lady played the piano, and four or five men performed on stringed instruments. The next day being Sunday I attended

---

* Why should a man be limited to one wife? I think he might be allowed to have two! but the English, as a rule, have peculiar ideas about matrimony, not even considering it to be right for a man to marry his deceased wife's sister.

† A *real* is the fourth part of a *peseta*, about 2½d. Spaniards often calculate in this way, which is rather puzzling.

the service in the English chapel. The clergyman was very young; I should say he had only recently been ordained; nevertheless, he had a good idea of preaching. In the afternoon I paid another visit to the promenade and saw a really fine turn out of carriages and horses, and a pleasing display of female beauty. The ladies seemed this day to be not afraid of showing themselves, and certainly some of them were remarkably handsome. In the evening I was accosted by a girl having in her hand a plate with a sheet of paper upon it, which she held out to me in a supplicating manner. This was the certificate she had *purchased* from the Government to enable her to beg. These beggars are very polite, and kiss the coin you have given them.

Before leaving this charming city, I thought I must, for the idea of the thing, get one of the numerous "barbers of Seville" to cut my hair, and as I could discover no descendant of *Figaro* carrying on the business of his illustrious ancestor, I dropped into a French hair-dresser's, and am thankful to be able to relate that my barber did his work well and played no trick upon me as once did an Englishman transacting business in the same capacity. This mischievous man, taking advantage of my being in a drowsy condition, having been lulled into that state by the soothing influence of the hair brush, proceeded to clip my moustache, and when I became thoroughly alive to the situation I found myself in the same frame of mind as *Samson* must have been in after *Delilah* and the Philistines had cut off his hair. But this was not to be compared to what I once read about in an English newspaper: There were two men courting the same lass; one, at all events was a tailor, I think, not a barber; the other possessed a fine flowing moustache; so the tailor in a spirit of sweet revenge took his shears and clipped off *one end* of his rival's moustache. The latter took action in a police-court and recovered damages.

All through this Spanish tour I found no English daily paper taken in at the hotels but the *Times*. As this journal costs three-pence I consider it a bad plan to subscribe to it, for one is able for the same sum to obtain *three* other papers; and the *Times* too is not a paper to be relied on. Apart from its forged letters I have in other matters caught it publishing false intelligence, and I would advise foreign hotel-keepers to have nothing to do with it, but in its place to substitute three penny papers.

What may be remarked at SEVILLE is their custom of drying clothes on the house-tops; the roofs being flat as at CADIZ. Every Spanish town that I know, however small it may be, is disfigured by a *Bull-ring*. In conversation with a Spaniard at CADIZ I was delighted to hear the opinion expressed that bull-fighting is likely at a no distant date to become extinct.

They don't muzzle their dogs in *Spain*, they cut off their tails instead, and muzzle their donkeys.

It seems impossible hereabouts to obtain a decent box of matches. As a rule you find none at all in your rooms. I imagine as all Spaniards smoke cigarettes one is supposed to carry one's own matches. And when you ask for a box they give you those wax ones which either bend and won't light, or when you have managed to strike one with success, you run a very good chance of burning your fingers. As I drove through the streets of SEVILLE, at five o'clock in the morning, the air was so mild that I had no occasion to put on my overcoat. At GUADALCANAL we had a splendid prospect; there was a fine open country with lofty mountains afar off. What a delightful country this must be for a walking or riding tour! There is such a dearth of hedges, fences and walls that one might go pretty well wherever one pleased without meeting with any impediment. At one o'clock we arrived at ZAFRA where a line branches off to HUELVA. Here I found a refreshment-room. Just after three we got to MERIDA, famous for its Roman remains, and I hired a cart to take my luggage to the *Fonda de la Viuda de Segura*. This was a clean whitewashed little inn. I was given a large room communicating with another, the occupant of which had to pass through mine to get to his own. There were glass doors which divided these rooms and mine also from the dining-room, and these had muslin curtains through which, of course, one could see pretty clearly. Two sisters, *Maria* and *Rafaela*, very pretty girls, assisted by an elderly woman did the work of the house. *Maria* was about eighteen years of age, but *Rafaela* much younger, a regular little beauty, and as graceful as a Sylph. At dinner we numbered ten in all, and five of those present kept their hats on their heads throughout the meal. I was very much amused at a little incident that occurred. One of the party ordered a bottle of beer, this he offered to those about him, and each person *poured some of the beer* into *his wine* and then drank the mixture. They were a very merry lot.

The river *Guardiana* is of great breadth at MERIDA, but was mostly dried up when I was there. However, the women found water sufficient to enable them to carry out their ablutionary avocations. The following morning I looked about the place, and was agreeably surprised to find no

beggars. The night had been cold and ice was upon the
ground. From MERIDA back to OPORTO the route lay by
BADAJOZ, memorable for its siege, a picturesque town from the
distance, but dirty when one approaches it.

CONCLUDING REMARKS.

A FEW remarks on the journey from OPORTO to *England* may be of use or interest to some of my readers,
The train leaves OPORTO daily at eight a.m., and it is advisable for travellers to supply themselves with provisions for the first day's journey. There is a refreshment-room at REGOA which is passed between twelve and one o'clock, but not enough time is allowed to make a meal there. A stoppage of twenty minutes takes place at FREGENEDA, the frontier place in *Spain*, but the food there is not particularly nice; better is to be got at S. ESTEBAN, further on, but night has set in before we arrive at the last-named place. At MEDINA DEL CAMPO, where it is necessary to change trains, an hour or more is allowed, but MEDINA is not a good place for food. At 7.30 in the morning a short stop is made at MIRANDA when coffee is served, and SAN SEBASTIAN is reached before half-past eleven. However, I think it best to break the journey at HENDAYE, half-an-hour or more farther on; getting through the luggage examination (for HENDAYE is in *France*), and having a full twenty-four hours to stay there. Leave HENDAYE the next day at one p.m. and break the journey at ANGOULÊME. We arrived at ANGOULÊME at 9.15 p.m. and went to the *hotel de France*, an old-fashioned house in a good position in a garden of its own. *Balzac* was born in this house. The hotel is famous for *Paté de Perdreux* and such like delicacies; we also enjoyed excellent soup, an unusual thing in *France*, where, although *potage* is everywhere and at all times obtainable, it is seldom worth much. Old women, in thorough keeping with the establishment, did all the work, and generally the place was very comfortable. However, the shoe-cleaning was very badly done, and my sovereigns were only valued at twenty-four *francs* each.

All through *France*, the travelling was very dusty. I think it always is so—more so than in other countries. Leaving ANGOULÊME just before eleven a.m. you reach PARIS at about a quarter before six, and your best plan, if you only want to stay a night in the French metropolis, is to put up at the *Hotel du Chemin de Fer du Nord*. The cooking there is now excellent. Of course, these remarks apply only to those who travel by easy stages, and not to those going by the bi-weekly *sud* express.

APPENDIX I.

AVIGNON.

CAPITAL of Vaucluse . . . . . Before the revolution belonged to the Pope whose legate resided here, and it was the See of an Archbishop, erected in 1475. In the year 1309, the papal see was transferred to Avignon by Pope Clement V., and this city flourished about seventy years, the seat of the Roman Pontiff, and the metropolis of Christendom. By land, by sea, and the Rhone, the position of Avignon was on all sides accessible; the Southern provinces of France are not inferior even to Italy; new palaces arose for the accommodation of the Pope and Cardinals; and the arts of luxury were soon attracted by the treasures of the church. They were already possessed of the adjacent territory, the Venetian country, a populous and fertile spot, which had been ceded to the Popes in 1273, by Philip III., king of France; and the sovereignty of Avignon was afterwards purchased from the youth and distress of Jane, the first Queen of Naples and Countess of Provence, for the inadequate price of 80,000 florins. Under the shadow of the French monarchy, amidst an obedient people, the Popes enjoyed an honourable and tranquil state, to which they had long been strangers; but Italy deplored their absence, and Rome, in solitude and poverty, might repent of the ungovernable freedom which had driven from the Vatican the successor of St. Peter. As the old members of the sacred college died, it was filled with French cardinals, who beheld Rome and Italy with abhorrence and contempt, and perpetuated a series of national and even provincial Popes, attached with indissoluble ties to their native country. At length, the celebrated Petrarch warmly interested himself in restoring the Roman bishop to his ancient and peculiar diocese; and he addressed his exhortation to five successive Popes, with an eloquence that was inspired by the enthusiasm of sentiment and the freedom of language. Avignon, which had become the sink of sin and corruption, was the object of his abhorrence and contempt! and whilst he allowed that the successor of St. Peter was the Bishop of the Universal Church, he was of opinion that it was not on the banks of the Rhone but of the Tiber that the Apostle had fixed his everlasting throne. Since the removal of the Holy See, the sacred buildings of the Lateran and the Vatican, their altars and the saints, were left in a state of poverty and decay, and Rome was often painted under the image of a disconsolate matron. But it was alleged that the cloud which hung over the seven hills would be dispelled by the presence of their lawful sovereign ; eternal fame, the prosperity of Rome, and the peace of Italy, would be the recompense of the Pope, who should dare to embrace the generous resolution. Of the five Popes to whom Petrach addressed his exhortation, the three first, John XXII., Benedict XII., and Clement VI. were importuned or amused by the boldness of the orator; but the memorable change, which had been attempted by Urban V., between the years 1367 and 1370, was finally accomplished by Gregory XI., A.D. 1377, who did not survive his return to the Vatican above fourteen months. His decease was followed by the "Great Western Schism," which begun after the decease of Gregory XI. A.D. 1378 by the election of Clement VII. in opposition to Urban VI., and continued for about forty years, till the Council of Constance, A.D. 1414-1418, when the elevation of Martin V. was the era of the restoration and establishment of the Pope in the Vatican. During this interval there were two Popes, one residing in Rome or Italy and the other at Avignon.

APPENDIX II.

BARCELONA.

A RICH and strong city and seaport, in the province of Catalonia, of which it is the capital, and the See of a Bishop, Suffragen of the Archbishop of Taragona. It was originally founded by Hamilcar Barcar, the Father of Hanibal, and from him called "Barcino," about 250 years before Christ. It was reduced by the Romans, and continued subject to them till the kingdom of Spain was overrun by the Goths and Vandals, and afterwards by the Saracens and Moors. At the beginning of the ninth century it was possessed by the Moors under the government of Zade. This Governor having abused the clemency of Charlemagne, and by his perfidious behaviour provoked his son, Lewis, King of Aquitaine, Barcelona was invested, and the Generals, who were instructed with the command of the siege, had orders not to abandon it till Zade was delivered into the hands of Lewis. The Moor made an obstinate resistance, but finding it was impossible to preserve the city any longer, after a defence of many months, he determined to throw himself upon the Emperor's mercy, and was condemned to perpetual exile. At length, however, the city surrendered, and the King of Aquitaine appointed one Bera, Count of Barcelona. The city continued subject to him and his successors, who were distinguished by the titles of "Counts of Barcelona," from the year 802 to 1131, when it was united to the Crown of Arragon by the marriage of Don Raymond V., Count of Barcelona, with Donna Petronilla, the daughter of Don Ramiro, the monk, the heiress of Arragon. In consequence of the revolt of the Catalonians, in 1465, Barcelona was beseiged by Don Juan II., King of Arragon, in 1471. The siege was prosecuted for a considerable time with vigour, but without effect; however, in 1472 it capitulated on its own terms, and the king, upon his public entry into the city, confirmed all its privileges. In 1640, the Catalans having shaken off the yoke of the Spaniards, called in the French to their succour, and they continued masters of the capital till 1652, when after a siege of fifteen months, it surrendered to Don Juan of Austria. In 1697 it was again taken by the French, under the command of the Duke of Vendome, but

restored the same year to the Spaniards by the peace of
Ryswick. Although the inhabitants of Barcelona had taken
the oath of fidelity to the King of Spain, Philip V., and received from him a confirmation of their privileges, they
invited the English and Dutch, and the Governor was
obliged to surrender the town to the allies in 1705, when
Charles, afterwards Emperor, was received and proclaimed
king. In the following year, Philip, assisted by the French,
assailed the city, and took the fortress of Mont Jouy, but the
fleet of the allies advancing to the relief of the besieged, he
was compelled to abandon the enterprise and retire from the
place, May 12th, 1706. By the treaty of Utrecht, in 1713,
the troops of the Emperor evacuated Catalonia, but the inhabitants of Barcelona persisted in their revolt and would
not acknowledge Philip for their king. Accordingly they
suffered blockade for a year, which was followed by a terrible
bombardment, and at length, after a siege of sixty-two days
from the opening of the trenches, by the Duke of Berwick,
the town was taken by assault on the 11th of September,
1714. By the moderation of the conqueror the city was
saved from pillage, but the inhabitants were deprived of their
privileges; they have since, however, been re-established,
and in 1715 a citadel was erected to keep them in awe.

APPENDIX III.

LERIDA CARTHAGENIAN.

A TOWN in Catalonia, distinguished in ancient and modern history for the great events which have rendered it memorable; it was the capital of the country of the Ilergetas long before the first invasion of Spain by the Romans and had its own particular princes. In the plains of Lerida, Cipio gained a signal victory over Hanno, the Carthegenian General. It was likewise under the walls of this town that Julius Cæsar conquered the lieutenants of Pompey; the beauty of its situation and the fertility of the country, attracted the attention of the Romans, and as soon as they had made a conquest of it, they planted colonies there, and gave it the title of " Municipium Ilerdense ; " this town having fallen under the dominion of the Goths, embraced the Christian religion, and was the seat of a celebrated council held here, A.D. 528 or 524. A council held here in 546 is remarkable for two of its canons: one prohibiting ecclesiastics from shedding human blood, and another permitting the communion to be administered to magicians when they are dying. After the conquest of the Moors it became at first subject to the Caliphs of Damascus and afterwards to the Moorish kings of Cordoba, but its own Governor erecting the standard of rebellion and usurping the supreme power, it had a separate king. In 1149, Raymond Beringer, the last Count of Barcelona, who had just ascended the throne of Arragon, took Lerida from the Moors, and from that time it formed a part of Catalonia.

APPENDIX IV.

ZARAGOZA.

BY ancient Spanish authors written *Caragoça*, an ancient, large, and wealthy city, the capital of Arragon, was founded, as some have said by the Phœnicians, who gave it the name of *Salduba*, or *Saldinia* ; it was in a flourishing state under the Romans, and being colonized by Augustus it was called *Cæsarea* or *Cæsarea-Augusta*, of which the present name is a corruption. The Goths, conducted by Enric, their king, became masters of it about the year 470. The Saracens, under Musa, their General, drove the Goths from it in 712, and took possession in the name of the Caliph of Damascus, but in 753 it was taken by the Moor, Zugif, Governor-General of Spain. The inhabitants attempting to shake off the yoke of the new Empire formed a republic in 825, but they were soon compelled to implore the clemency of the Moorish king. At length, this town became, A.D. 1017, the capital of a small empire, about the time when the several governors in different parts of Spain usurped supreme power. The Governor of Saragosa assumed kingly power, and transmitted the crown to his posterity, who retained it till Alphonso I. King of Arragon, made himself master of the town in December 1115, after a siege of eight months; he then made it the capital of his kingdom, and the residence of the princes who succeeded him. It remained the capital of Arragon until that country became, in the sixteenth century, simply a province of the Spanish Monarchy by the marriage of its king, Ferdinand, the Catholic, with Isabella, heiress of the kingdoms of Leon and Castille. . . . . .
The church of Nuestra Dona del Pilar is a grand and superb building; the principal altar is in the Gothic style, constructed almost wholly of alabaster and exhibiting a mixture of different kinds of sculpture. The arts, it is said, have combined to decorate the interior of the church. In the centre of the cathedral there is one edifice which is strikingly beautiful. The principal front is a chapel of Our Lady of the Pillar, who appeared upon this very pillar to St. James, and afterwards gave to him the image which is worshipped at her altar. Over this there is a dome corresponding to the great dome under which it stands, serving by way of canopy

to the image of the Virgin. The three other fronts of this elegant tabernacle are in like manner chapels. Besides the great dome there are many smaller domes surrounding it, each with elegant paintings in compartments, the subjects of which are historical, taken from the sacred writings or from the legends of the saints, to whom the chapels and altars are dedicated. . . . . The wealth of the cathedral is inestimable in silver, gold, precious stones and rich embroidery, sent by all the Catholic Sovereigns of Europe, to deck its priests and to adorn its altars. Many of these presents being modern (1819) are worthy of attention for elegance as well as for the value of their pearls, diamonds, emeralds, and rubies. In a word, whatever wealth could command or human art could execute, has been collected to excite the admiration of all who view the treasures of the church.

APPENDIX V.

SALAMANCA.

OF all public edifices, the cathedral is the most worthy of notice; it is majestic and in the Gothic style. Its foundation was laid, A.D. 1515, but it was not finished till the year 1734. It is 378 feet in length, 181 feet wide in the clear, 130 feet high in the nave, and 80 feet in the aisles. The whole is beautiful; but the most striking part of this church, and of many public buildings in this city, is the sculpture, which displays much taste, and is well preserved. Over the principal gate is represented, in bold relief, the Adoration of the Sages, and over another, the public entrance of Christ into Jerusalem, all appearing as fresh and sharp as if they were recently put up. Besides the chief gate, which is finally executed, it has a superb and grand steeple surrounded by a broad commodious and handsome gallery where several people can walk abreast. . . . . . The University was founded in the year 1200, by Alphonso IX., King of Leon, and regulated by Alphonso the Wise, A.D. 1254. It soon rose to importance and became eminent in Europe by acquaintance with the Arabian authors, and through them with the Greek. The reverence of its first professors for Aristotle and for Thomas Aquinas, it is said, continous to the present day, La Bude dates the establishment of this University in the year 1239 out of the ruins of that of Palencia, and he says there have been as many as 8,000 scholars in it, who came hither from every part of Spain, and 7,000 from the other countries of Europe. But this number has been since much reduced.

APPENDIX VI.

" Now kepe you fro the white and fro the rede,
" Namely fro the white wine of Lepe,
" That is to sell in Fish Street and in Chepe ;
" This wine of Spain crepeth subtelly.
" And other wines growing fast by,
" Of which riseth such fumosite
" That when a man hath dronk draughts thre,
" And weneth that he be at home in Chepe
" He is in Spain, right at the town of Lepe."

From Chaucer's Prologue—*The Pardoner's Tale*

www.ingramcontent.com/pod-product-compliance
Lightning Source LLC
Chambersburg PA
CBHW022133160426
43197CB00009B/1265